Angus Mackay

Queensland (Australia) : The Exhibits and Exhibitors and

Description of the Colony

Angus Mackay

Queensland (Australia) : The Exhibits and Exhibitors and Description of the Colony

ISBN/EAN: 9783743338913

Manufactured in Europe, USA, Canada, Australia, Japa

Cover: Foto ©ninafisch / pixelio.de

Manufactured and distributed by brebook publishing software
(www.brebook.com)

Angus Mackay

Queensland (Australia) : The Exhibits and Exhibitors and

Description of the Colony

QUEENSLAND

(AUSTRALIA.)

THE EXHIBITS AND EXHIBITORS,

AND

DESCRIPTION OF THE COLONY.

BRISBANE:

BY AUTHORITY: JAMES C. BEAL, GOVERNMENT PRINTER,

WILLIAM STREET.

1878.

TABLE OF CONTENTS.

QUEENSLAND AS IT IS.

BY ANGUS MACKAY.

Queensland, as will be seen from the accompanying map, is a section of Australia. It is a colony of absolutely free people, who make and administer their own laws. It occupies the north-eastern portion of the great island continent of Australia, and is of immense extent. Seventeen years only have passed since the colony was first founded, as separate from its older neighbour, New South Wales; but during that short time the population has grown from 32,000, in 1860, to close upon 200,000 in 1878. There is room and occupation in the colony for millions of industrious people. The few there make employment for the many. This is exemplified in the fact that, although in its natural state, the land offers no subsistence to the white man—such as he has been used to—yet, soon as they have arrived, the thousands of people who come every year find employment for themselves and their capital in Queensland.

The greater portion of the colonists are of British origin; they have come from England, Scotland, and Ireland. But there are many also from the continent of Europe and from America, and at the present day the children of these immigrants make up a large proportion of the whole population. The laws of the colony are based upon those of Great Britain, but are framed and administered so as to apply to the conditions of a new country· There are no hindrances whatever to the full enjoyment of citizenship by all who respect the laws.

The area of Queensland is computed at 430,000,000 of acres, or about 174,000,000 hectares, French measurement. There is great variety of soil, formation, and aspect in a territory so vast. In size Queensland is eleven times as large as England. There is considerable variety of climate, although in that particular Australia does not compare with European experience. The latitudinal space occupied by Queensland is from 29° S. to 10° S., and the longitudinal space from 138° E. to 153° E.; yet the whole of this immense range has a climate similar almost to that of Southern Europe. A very large proportion of Queensland, in so far as climate is concerned, compares almost closely with the south of France, with Spain, and with Portugal. The summer is warm as that of Louisiana in the United States, or of the island of Cuba ; but, even now, while the country is still new, and comparatively unreclaimed, there is not the liability to climatic and epidemic disease which affect white people in the former country, nor the lassitude and loss of energy which attacks them in the latter. Queensland, all over the territory, is a healthy country ; the white races do not degenerate there.

Many rivers—several of them noble streams and avenues for ocean traffic—open out to the sea. Among them may be mentioned the Brisbane, the Mary, Burnett, Fitzroy, Pioneer, and Herbert, on all of which are growing town and cities, of which further information is given in this essay. None of the navigable rivers open back to such distance from the coast as might be expected in so great an extent of country ; the formation of Australia precludes this. A range of mountains, rising to an elevation of over 2,000 feet above sea level, runs, for long distances, almost parallel with the coast. The rivers named, and many others, have their source in these mountains. On the land or western side of this great Dividing Range, are vast plains, and immense stretches of soil as rich as any on earth. The coast country also is rich in quality of soil, but it is more broken and rugged than the elevated western country.

The Brisbane River is navigable for fully 80 miles, and the Mary, Fitzroy, and other rivers are navigable for nearly as long distances. Steam vessels, and merchant ships carrying passengers and freight, come up the towns on these rivers and discharge their cargoes.

On the coast country—from Moreton Bay, which is close to the southern boundary of Queensland, to Cape York, the most northerly point in Australia, and still within the Queensland territory—are many harbours, each with its settlement, less or more populous. The coast country is thus dotted with settlements along its whole extent, with long intervals between. But every year adds to the places occupied and breaks in upon the solitude of the unoccupied spaces.

Railways are being pushed in from the seaboard towns to the interior, in order to bring down the heavy products of the country—wool, tallow, hides, minerals, coal, &c., and to provide facilities for an increasing passenger traffic. Already 357 miles of railway are open for business, and the Parliament of the colony have authorised the construction of 345 miles in addition. The lines already at work connect the capital, Brisbane, with the rich Darling Downs and the country lying westerly ; the second line open connects the Port of Rockhampton with the country lying westerly and northerly. New lines are being surveyed from Maryborough, Bundaberg, and Townsville, and extensions are being added to the older lines. These railways are all Government works, and are managed and controlled by Government officers.

From the ports and towns on the coast, there are roads and tracks running into the interior of the country. (*See tables of distances at pages* 27, 28.) It is indicative of the character of the people that, at even this early stage, when the greater extent of the roads of the country are mere tracks, with no more in the way of road-making done to them than the partial clearing away of the indigenous timber; and even before that is accomplished that mails are carried on horseback and in vehicles literally all over the country; and that already townships of 2,000 inhabitants, and many that have not one half of that population are connected by electric telegraph. Messages of ten words are sent anywhere within the colony over these telegraph lines for 1s. The rate of postage all over the colony is 2d., and newspapers are carried free.

Rainfall and Climate.

Local formation, and the position of mountains and rivers have considerable effect upon the rainfall and upon climate in Queensland. Taking the rainfall as a guide, there is no part of the colony that can be considered arid, in the general sense of that term. The heaviest rainfall is on the coast lands, where in places it averages 90 inches. Further inland there is less rainfall; but the least upon record, viz., 18 inches of rain for the year at Dalby, at 120 miles from the sea, is a rainfall quite sufficient for any operations in agriculture, mining, or manufactures that may be carried on. Statistics regarding rainfall and temperature are chronicled with great care by an officer specially detailed for that purpose. His records give the following results in rainfall :—

Locality.			Latitude.	Rain, Inches.	Rainy Days.
Cape Moreton	...	...	27° S.	70	120
Brisbane	...	...	27½° S.	45	119
Maryborough	...	...	25½° S.	34	89
Sandy Cape	...	...	24¾° S.	49	132
Keppel Bay	...	...	23⅓° S.	38	41
Rockhampton	...	...	23⅓° S.	41	74
Mackay	...	...	21° S.	68	110
Bowen	...	...	20° S.	39	80
Townsville	...	...	19¼° S.	33	71
Cardwell	...	...	18¼° S.	90	117
Vale Herbert	...	...	18° S.	64	118

Ascending from the coast to the table land, a change becomes apparent, as shown by the following table :—

Locality.	Miles from Sea.	Rain, Inches.	Rainy Days.
Ipswich	30	40	100
Gympie Diggings ...	30	23	66
Westwood	45	27	49
Nebo	50	22½	49
Helidon	60	24	49
Toowoomba	80	27	132
Ravenswood	70	20	38
Banana	80	22	50
Warwick	90	25	58
Dalby	112	18	50
Clermont	130	29	30
Taroom	160	25	70

Toowoomba is 1,900 feet above the sea level, at the eastern edge of the Main Range, 61 inches of rain fell in that town during 164 days.

Warwick, 1,500 feet high, averaged, during seven years, 32 inches in 67 days. Springsure, at the same elevation as Warwick, but seventy miles further from the ocean, had a mean, from seven years' observation, of 24 inches in 46 days. While but 14 inches fell in 1865, 45 fell in 1870.

Further west from the Main Range the rain is less.

Locality.	Miles from Sea.	Rain, Inches.	Rainy Days.
Condamine	180	18	47
Mount Hutton	180	15	29
Roma	230	13	62

The prevailing winds of Queensland account materially for the salubrity and healthy character of the climate. What are known as "hot winds" in other parts of Australia, are scarcely known here. This is accounted for by the fact that, as these winds come from the interior of the country, they do not encounter arid barren wastes, but immense stretches of grassed or timber country, in which their fierce heat is tempered. From a record kept in Brisbane, the prevailing winds are seen to be, during the number of days given :—north, 49 ; north-west, 39 ; west, 76 ; east, 94 ; south-west, 159; south, 205; south-east, 218 ; north-east, 232. The winds blowing off the land interior stand at 274, to 649 from off the seaboard. The northerly winds, from the equator, are as 320 to 582 blowing from the south pole. Thus it is that the winds conduce to the salubrity of the Queensland climate, and disarm it of the evils experienced in other tropical and sub-tropical countries.

Agriculture.

There is great diversity in the agriculture of Queensland. The coast country is decidedly semi-tropical, and the productions are in bulk of that kind. The sugar-cane, maize, cotton, the sweet potatoe, yams, and a host of other semi-tropical products come to the highest perfection, and great skill has already been acquired in working crops of the kind referred to. But the experience of fifteen or sixteen years in cultivating for these products has taught the colonists that there are exceptions in what has proven to be the general course of proceeding. Local formation has much to do with the climate in places separate but a few miles. Thus we find, on the Brisbane River, farms on which sugar-cane has been cultivated for years without any attacks or injury from frost. And again, and in places further north (and that ought to be, from position, still more tropical), there are places on which the cane has failed by reason of attacks of frost with yearly persistency. These differences go to make up what is known as "colonial experience," and which new arrivals in the country would do well to make themselves acquainted with.

On these same coast lands, the vine, and fruits of various kinds, from the banana to the peach, are grown. With the exception of vine culture, to which much careful attention has been devoted, gardening is comparatively in its infancy in the country. Of late years, Chinese gardeners have come in, and so successful has their system of heavily watering become, that they have nearly gained a monopoly of the market garden business. It was so in California in former years, but the settlement in that country of large bodies of French and Italian gardeners, has disturbed the Chinese. The men from Europe brought wind mills, pumps, and other machinery to their aid, and they have displaced the Celestials. And when a similar system is followed here there shall be similar results.

The Sugar-Cane.

This, as an agricultural product, has taken the lead of all others in Queensland. It is comparatively a new industry, although so well established. Prior to 1866, all the sugar grown in the country, was in botanical or in private gardens. Plantations were first formed in the Moreton Bay District, near the southern border of the colony. Then others were formed in the Maryborough District, and further north in the Herbert District, and an entirely new district named the Mackay, with the Pioneer River as an outlet to the sea, has been devoted entirely to the production of sugar, and has taken the lead of all other parts of the colony in that article. There are now about eighty sugar manufactories in Queensland, and some 16,000 acres of land under sugar-cane. The average return per acre of sugar is a shade over one ton. To make a ton of sugar requires, on an average from 16 to 18 tons of cane. Where the cultivation is really good, and the cane well farmed, the quality is better, and 14 to 15 tons of cane yield one ton of sugar. From the improvement going on in the manufacture, still better returns are obtained every year. The cane crop of 1876-7 was, in so far as quality went, about the best ever reaped in Queensland.

Report from the French Islands.

In 1875, the writer was commissioned to proceed to the French West India Islands, Martinique, Gaudaloupe, and their dependencies, and report upon the system of cane farming and sugar manufacturing followed there. That system, known as the French central factory system, separates the growing of cane from the manufacture of sugar as completely as the growing of wheat is separated from the milling of flour. The process has been eminently successful in the French islands, and, it is believed, would be equally successful here. The mill owners in Queensland would gladly welcome a class of persons such as farm the lands of Martinique—persons with sufficient capital to cultivate to maturity from 20 to 100 acres of cane. They would find here many mill owners who would allow them the use of land for a very small rental, and who would contract to purchase all the cane they could grow, at prices equal to those paid to the cane farmers of Martinique, or about ten shillings per ton. The yield of cane here, per acre, is as heavy as on the islands; were equally careful farming applied to the cane, the returns would be heavier. Crops of from 50 to 60 tons per acre have been grown here; 30 tons per acre is not a heavy crop. In the islands 25 tons per acre is a fair crop. The belief is that those West Indian cane farmers would do well here. They would very soon be able to purchase land of their own, as will be more fully explained under the headings relating to that division of our subject.

Distilling.

Distilling from molasses and cane refuse is carried on somewhat largely. There are twelve distilleries in the various sugar districts of the colony. Their products are a colonial spirit about 20 o.p., and also pure spirit of wine. Distilling from the grape and from grape refuse is also a colonial industry. In the latter case, brandy is the product aimed at, but in this branch, as well as the other relating to distilling from cane refuse, there is much scope for the introduction of skill and improvements.

Cane Farming—Sugar-Making.

Into the minutiæ of cane-farming there is no intention to
enter, very full particulars are obtainable from volumes printed
in Queensland. Here it will suffice to say that the very richest
alluvial and volcanic soils are selected for cane. In Queensland
these new fresh soils are very rich. The land at first is
covered with timber, which is cleared off at a cost of from
£3 to £7 per acre. The land is then prepared as for wheat.
Furrows are opened with a plough or hoe, from 5 to 7 feet
apart, and in these furrows cane plants—usually the tops or
joints about 12 inches long—are laid. The distance between the
plants varies from one to three feet. From three to a dozen
canes spring from each plant. The cultivation of the crop is
almost similar to that of maize or Indian corn; the soil is kept
very clean and loose between the rows of cane. This planting
is carried on from October to April. The crop is ready for
cutting in from twelve to eighteen months after planting. The
quantity cut depends upon the state of the soil, its quality, and
the style of farming. Sixty tons per acre is a heavy yield;
twenty tons a light yield. Until recently, the mill-owners calcu-
lated on growing their own cane; now many of the best of them
are desirous of encouraging farmers to take to this business and
to grow cane for sale to the mills. Very capital machinery has
been placed on the majority of plantations, but the planters, to
a man, are desirous of improving their modes of manufacture.
There is a large market for sugars in the colonies, and, until that
is supplied, there will be no risk of overdoing the sugar business
in Australia.

Cotton.

Previous to the cultivation of sugar upon an extensive scale,
cotton was a favourite crop in Queensland. During the latter
years of the American war, when prices were extra high, cotton
was a leading product of the colony; but as prices fell, the area
under cotton decreased. The quantity grown now is small, and
is confined to the West Moreton District.

The quality of cotton grown in Queensland is very superior.
The yield per acre also is satisfactory, being as heavy as that
grown in the best districts of the United States, or from 200 to
400 lbs. of clean, ginned fibre per acre. The planting season, in
Queensland, extends from September to December. The season
of growth is long, there being no decisive or killing frost here
to injure the strength of the staple. Picking is carried on
during the winter season, from April to July, and at this time
the most serious drawback experienced in cotton production was
felt. During April and May heavy rains are experienced, which,

when they occurred, were against cotton picking. But the supposition is that when this industry moves ahead again, there will be alterations attempted in the time of sowing and picking. It was found that the plant is perennial here, grows over more than one season, and that it is profitable to secure a second crop by pruning back the first year's plants, and inducing a fresh growth from the roots. In other respects the cultivation of cotton, and its preparation for export, are similar to the process followed in America. There is published information in the colony, giving full details of the production of cotton.

Maize—Indian Corn.

This crop is grown on the elevated as well as the lower coast lands. Maize comes to the fullest perfection in Queensland, and heavy crops are gathered. There are two sowing seasons, and two crops are gathered annually. The first is sown in August or September, and the second during December or January. The crop takes from four to five months to come to maturity. It yields from 30 to 80 bushels (56 lbs. per bushel) of shelled corn per acre. The seed, selected from the best cobs of the previous year's growth, are dropped in furrows or in holes about 3 x 4 feet apart. As the plants spring up the surface soil has to be kept loose and clean. The ears when ripe, are pulled from the stalks by hand. But in the shelling and cleaning, Machinery aids the farmer. Machinery of the very best type known in America has been introduced to Queensland, and will aid materially in increasing the corn crop.

Over 35,000 acres of land are under maize in Queensland, but so great is the demand for this grain, in order to supply the immense numbers of horses working on the goldfields, on the roads and railways, that Queensland barely supplies what is necessary for her own consumption. But the cultivation is extending, and it is expected that, ere many years, the production of pork from corn will become a large colonial industry. There is room for it.

Wheat, Barley, Oats.

These grains all do well on the elevated lands, west of the Main Range, and fairly well on the coast lands. In the districts of Toowoomba, Allora, and Warwick alone (see rain and weather tables pages 3 and 4 for distance) about 5,000 acres are devoted to wheat. There are very excellent flour mills in all those districts, capable of grinding all the wheat that shall be grown for years. The process of farming wheat is precisely similar to that followed in Europe. April and May are the sowing seasons. The harvest is during October and November. From 25 to 30 bushels (bushel, about 64 lbs.) per acre is the average crop. The quality of the grain is very excellent. During 1877, reaping machinery was introduced that binds as well as cuts wheat and barley in the field. This harvesting, owing to the impossibility of getting experienced hands when they were required, has hitherto been a serious obstacle against wheat farming, but with the aid of the machinery now available this branch of farming is expected to extend rapidly.

Barley is grown for brewing purposes, and also for export ; and oats mostly for cutting green, or for making hay, for which there is a continuous demand for horse feed.

The extent of other farming products are summarised in the following tabular statement compiled from official records : the figures refer to acres :—

The progress of Farming in Queensland from 1866 to 1876.

Year.	Wheat.	Maize.	Potatoes.	Cotton.	Sugar Cane.	Tobacco.	Bananas.*	Pineapples.*	Vines.	Gardens.	Miscellan.†	Total.
1866 ...	2,566	9,930	1,587	2,884	607	19	...	...	202	1,550	5,088	24,433
1867 ...	6,657	10,598	1,912	8,149	1,995	8	...	...	194	1,884	4,162	31,559
1868 ...	3,783	12,663	2,027	11,453	3,396	24	331	135	333	1,569	3,607	39,321
1869 ...	3,083	16,114	1,814	14,426	5,165	22	334	195	322	1,569	3,990	47,034
1870 ...	3,021	16,382	2,627	14,674	6,341	18	339	179	414	1,728	6,487	52,210
1871 ...	3,247	20,682	3,121	12,962	9,581	62	389	169	430	2,214	7,112	59,969
1872 ...	3,842	21,377	2,837	12,002	11,757	52	233	97	391	1,852	8,051	62,491
1873 ...	3,745	21,414	3,069	9,663	14,495	26	275	141	364	1,845	9,181	64,218
1874 ...	3,810	31,356	3,316	4,149	14,600	29	331	131	413	1,928	10,263	70,931
1875 ...	4,478	38,711	3,056	1,674	13,459	74	243	86	376	1,918	13,132	77,347
1876 ...	5,700	41,707	3,928	573	13,690	59	345	151	523	2,610	...	85,569

* Information as to the area under these crops not collected until 1868.

† Under this heading (Miscellaneous) are included the following crops, viz.:—Barley Oats, Rye, Millet, Sorghum, Arrowroot, Sown Grasses, &c., &c.

Live Stock.

Queensland is a rich pastoral country ; the leading occupations of the population are connected with sheep, cattle, and horses. The western country—described as elevated, and sloping gently away westerly from the great Dividing Range—is, with the exception of the wheat-growing districts already named, devoted entirely to pastoral pursuits. The extent of the business classed under this heading may be understood from the following details of the live stock in the various districts of the colony at the end of 1875-6 :—

Districts.	Horses.	Cattle.	Sheep.	Pigs.
Banana...	1,311	31,474	123,185	73
Blackall	2,706	32,731	491,645	113
Bowen	2,223	60,133	13,520	732
Brisbane	6,394	37,804	6,354	6,321
Bundaberg	949	17,257	1,350	1,521
Burke	1,414	41,400	12,230	50
Cardwell and Somerset	857	8,324	657	110
Charleville	2,563	36,680	581,114	398
Charters Towers and ⎰ Cape River ... ⎰	1,568	44,559	18,487	579
Clermont & Copperfield	3,057	25,957	823,837	965
Cook	756	1,003	900	501
Condamine	1,238	10,626	91,909	134
Cunnamulla	4,870	211,082	76,269	136
Dalby	3,535	20,650	351,450	892
Etheridge	922	23,864	...	13
Fort Cooper	522	9,943	49,160	49
Gatton	2,910	27,534	3,542	2,095
Gayndah	2,897	64,736	231,482	257
Gladstone and Kroombit	2,100	98,784	39,632	312
Goodna	910	6,044	232	697
Goondiwindi	1,389	14,401	105,037	121
Gympie	2,426	41,324	16,489	1,178
Inglewood	1,473	20,983	78,723	39
Ipswich	9,427	80,767	70,449	7,149
Leyburn	747	8,214	59,911	158
Logan	4,164	50,775	1,533	3,219
Mackay	2,022	30,597	395	718
Marathon	2,153	60,953	273,197	18
Maryborough	4,348	59,953	2,209	3,125
Nanango	1,516	32,900	34,175	130
Palmer	953	3,219	...	193
Ravenswood	470	7,325	1,537	215
Rawbelle	282	25,314	25,170	20
Rockhampton	7,461	122,787	12,240	3,510
Roma	4,352	53,357	612,181	421
St. George	5,023	111,292	174,844	255
St. Lawrence	2,095	41,192	86,014	296
Springsure	2,705	24,675	615,885	236
Stanthorpe	1,490	12,707	112,759	638
Surat	1,376	26,188	103,880	212
Tambo	631	7,700	46,093	92
Taroom	2,871	26,028	305,644	78
Tenningering	1,550	59,315	15,795	591
Toowoomba	7,032	28,726	966,076	3,959
Townsville	2,762	34,241	1,932	518
Warwick and Allora ...	7,077	26,094	588,652	3,411
Total	121,497	1,812,576	7,227,774	46,447

The totals of Live Stock in 1876, were: Horses, 133,625; cattle, 2,079,979; sheep, 7,315,074; pigs, 53,455.

Sheep and Wool.

The greatest interest of all, it will be seen, is connected with sheep. They are kept on immense sheep walks or "runs." The flocks on these runs vary from 5,000 to 100,000. Some sheep owners have more than 100,000, and their possessions, partly purchased land and partly leased from the Government for merely nominal rents, are counted by tens and twenties and hundreds of square miles. The Merino sheep is most in favour; fully 90 per cent. of all the sheep in Queensland are of Merino blood; many of the flocks are very fine, especial care and great expense having been incurred in perfecting an Australian Merino type, the wool of which is famous all over the world. The Merino is bred for wool alone, although in point of quality it is a fair mutton yielder. But the carcass is light, and to obtain a sheep more to the mind of butchers, Leicester, Romney Marsh, Cheviot, and other larger framed breeds have been introduced. The experience of fully twelve years, during all of which time the heavier breeds have been crossed with the Merino, as bred pure, proves that, in Queensland, sheep of all kinds, both full and cross bred, reach the fullest perfection and weight. The heavier kinds of sheep are mainly bred near the towns, where both the squatters (or large sheep owners, who lease land) and selectors (who own from 100 to 5,000 acres) breed and cross the heavier sheep for the butchers.

As stated, Australian Merino wool has a fame and an excellence peculiar to itself, and is recognised by woollen manufacturers all over the world. At the great American Exhibition at Philadelphia in 1876, the wool of Queensland received the highest honors from the judges of all nations who examined it both scientifically and practically. At this exhibition in Paris, the exhibits of wool are not so numerous as at Philadelphia, but being nearer to the greater markets of Europe, to which the exports of Australia are sent, there will be every opportunity for putting the staple of Queensland to such tests as may be requisite.

For the double purpose of making the freight light as possible, and in order to present their staple in as perfect state as possible, a large proportion of the wool of Queensland is washed while upon the living sheep and before it is shorn. Australians excell in this art of wool washing. With them it is a science, and vast capital and skill are applied to it. The sheep, as a commencement of the washing process, are first sprinkled with water, while in close warm sheds. This is to loosen the dirt on their fleeces, and to raise the temperature of their bodies. They are next put into a large tank of warm water, containing soap, and occasionally chemical ingradients of a cleaning character. After being soaked, the sheep are brought, one at a time, under what are termed "spouts"—in reality, thin streams of water discharged with heavy pressure through a crack-like split. The effect is instantaneous. The sheep, from a muddy dirty colour, are made white as snow. After a time, and after being allowed to dry, they are shorn. From 2,000 to 3,000 sheep are washed daily at the large wash-pools of Queensland. The Merino yields from 2½ to 5 lbs. of the clean wool shown in the Queensland department. In its dirty or greasy state, this wool weighs from 5 to 10 lbs. per head.

The questions are common, "To what extent can this wool business be carried in Australia? How many sheep is the country capable of supporting?" In 1876 the number, as shown by the official records, and they are very carefully prepared, was over 7,000,000 for Queensland. Ninety-nine per cent. of this number are, and always have been, grazed on the indigenous grasses of the country. As an average, it may be accepted that one sheep represents three acres of this grazing land. But one acre of cultivated grasses, in Queensland, is equal to the support of three sheep. Cultivation and the growing of grasses are now amongst the improvements carried on by pastoralists as well as the farming community; and as cultivation increases, should the demand for wool be sufficient, it is quite within the bounds of possibility that Queensland can support 20,000,000 of sheep.

Those selectors and holders of small areas of ground, or say from 500 to 5,000 arpents, and who graze from 200 to 3,000 sheep, are a very prosperous portion of the community of Queensland, and there is every inducement to increase the number.

Cattle and Horses.

The numbers, respectively, in the colony, are 133,625 horses, and 2,079,979 cattle. Both classes of stock are kept in large mobs on stations. Like the owners of large mobs of sheep, these great cattle and horse owners, are named squatters. Short-horn cattle are most in favour, and there has been no backwardness in devoting enterprise, skill, and capital to the improving of the breed. Bulls of the very best blood are imported. The Hereford and Devon breeds have also received attention, and are in the colony in sufficient numbers to judge of there suitability, and there is a strong desire to introduce the best breeds of dairy stock.

Considerable attention has been devoted to the breeding of horses, both heavy and light stock, for draught, coaching and riding purposes. The climate would seem to favour the latter most. The saddle horses of the country are famous for sound-ness, capacity for work, and durability. Numbers of Australian horses are shipped to India, and used there for artillery and cavalry purposes. It is but correct to say that they have no superiors for such work.

Great numbers of sheep, cattle and horses are still run in mobs in the open country, attended to by shepherds and stockmen; but it is becoming common for the squatters and selectors to fence in their lands. They fence with posts of timber, having four to seven strong iron wires passing through the posts. This makes a strong and durable fence. Paddocks, or enclosures fenced in this way, containing from 5,000 to 30,000 acres, are attended to by boundary riders and stockmen, who are all day in the saddle. Under the care of overseers, a superintendent, and the squatter himself, these men attend, during all but the shearing season amongst sheep, and the branding time for cattle and horses, to all the duties of station life.

Meat Preserving.

The preserved meat of Australia has won a high reputation in England, and deserves to be better known on the Continent of Europe. Exhibits from the colony are amongst those on view, and they will be tested during the time of the exhibition. This meat is prepared from the sheep and cattle brought in from the stations or runs described. No meat in the world is produced under more favourable and health giving circumstances. In the meat preserving establishments vast capital and skill have been brought to bear upon this industry, and no effort is spared in order to have the sheep and cattle killed, and the meat put up and presented to consumers in the very best manner that science and patient practice can suggest.

How the Lands are obtained.

In order to suit the various classes who desire to occupy the lands, regulations are framed, based upon Acts of the Legislature of the colony. These Acts provide for the leasing or renting, as well as the absolute selling of land for pastoral purposes ; and also for planting sugar-cane, and for the various phases of agriculture that have developed in Queensland. The leased pastoral lands are valued at fixed periods. The rents paid may be stated as ranging from one farthing to one penny per acre per annum. The leases are fixed for specified terms, and are regular articles of sale, as between the holder and purchaser, without any government interference whatever. They are sold and exchanged as the sheep, and live stock grazing on the leased lands are disposed of.

Lands are sold by the government, for agricultural purposes, at from 5s. to £3 per acre, according to the location, quality, and assumed value of the land. The payments may be in the lump, or may extend over five or ten years, a fixed proportion being paid annually to officers who attend to such matters alone, and who are able to give advice to persons who may desire to purchase land that is available in their several localities.

Lands that have been improved, are always for sale by private owners, and very often it is better for the new arrival to purchase these improved lands, through trustworthy agents, rather than select new and unimproved land.

Mining.—Gold.

Mining for gold, and copper, and tin, and coal, and a host of the minerals used in arts, and manufactures, are amongst the great industries of Queensland.

In order to illustrate the extent to which gold has been found in the colony, during the nine years since the discovery of gold at Gympie, in 1868, a pyramid is erected amidst the Queensland exhibits. This illustrates a bulk mass weighing more than two million ounces; and worth more than seven million pounds sterling, or more than one hundred and fifty millions of francs.

A large proportion of this gold was obtained by merely washing it free from the soil in which it was imbedded, from the surface to a depth of 30 feet. But the greater bulk of the gold is obtained in a much more difficult and scientific manner. This latter kind of gold is incorporate in quartz and in various other kinds of stone, sometimes in little particles and flakes, but more generally in such specks as the unaided eye cannot detect. Gold thus mixed is found in veins of from a few inches to ten feet, and occasionally greater width. These veins dip down into the earth, generally encased at each side by stone of the very hardest kind. Blasting powders, and the steel tools and machinery of the miner are used for following the veins of gold yielding stone, down, down 100 feet, 200, 400, 1,000 1,600 feet. The work is hard and continuous. Occasionally the prizes are heavy; but the great body of miners work hard for wages no higher than other occupations pay; and the great mass of the capital employed yields no more than a fair interest for the money expended and the risks run.

But mining is an absorbing pursuit, and those engaged in it, as employers and on their own account, follow the business steadily and with avidity. The value of machinery in Queensland for grinding quartz and extracting gold, is over £130,000.

The main gold yielding districts of Queensland are Gympie, the Palmer, the Etheridge, the Gilbert, Charters Towers, Cape River, Ravenswood, and Enoggera, from which specimens are exhibited.

Copper Mining.

There are immense deposits of Copper-bearing ores in Queensland. At Peak Downs, and at Mount Perry, work has been carried on extensively for many years. Both districts, indeed all the copper deposits as yet discovered, are distant from the coast and from water carriage, and, consequently, the cost of freighting this bulky heavy metal to places of shipment, has been a serious draw back to the industry. Railways must reach the mines before capital and labour can secure that full reward to which they are entitled in this business; and railways are projected as devised. The exhibits from Peak Downs Mine and from the Mount Perry Mine, prove the high quality of the metal.

Tin.

Early during 1872 tin ore was discovered near the southern border of Queensland, at a distance of about 120 miles from the coast. The first ore that was brought into Brisbane for examination and analysis looked like coarse black sand. For some time previously deposits of this "heavy black sand" were known to exist there, and were the subject of much speculation. When the deposits proved to be stream tin ore of the very richest description, there arose a rush, a regular stampede to the country bearing a metal of so much value. The laws of Queensland make provision for any person taking up portions of land, or selections to work minerals. A demand for the lands in question arose at once, and thousands of acres were selected.

The tin ore was at first found in deposits in the beds of the creeks. The country is of a granite formation, and although an elevated table-land, it is much broken and cut up by watercourses. Thousands of men from all parts of Australia were soon at work, they stripped off the surface soil, or scooped up the deposits from holes in the creeks, and by washing, the tin ore was separated from the other and much lighter earthy substances. Soon as it dried the ore was put up in bags and sent to Brisbane.

At first, there was, when the ore reached England, a disposition to underrate its value. The colonists then went into smelting and refining. Until 1876, when the price for tin fell to the low rate at which it is still selling, there was a large business done in tin, and large tracts of country were found to yield ore. Since then this branch of mining has not been so brisk. About 100 tons of ore came, weekly from the mines, and this quantity seems as much as a market can be readily obtained for. In Queensland the ore has been taken from the creek beds and from watercourses, into which the metal has, in ages past, been drifted. But the belief is that there are reefs of tin ore, and great heavy deposits from which the ligher particles unearthed as yet have been washed downwards. The tin mining industry has given rise to the busy town of Stanthorpe, in a locality where at the commencement of 1872 there were no prospects whatever of a township.

Coal.

Queensland has immense deposits of coal, and mines are worked in the West Moreton, Darling Downs, and Burnett districts. Specimens of the products of these mines are exhibited, and show a soft coal of fair quality for steam making and domestic purposes. The supply is already more than sufficient for the purposes of colonists, and exports are made to the other colonies, to the East, and to California. As yet, the surface coal seems to have sufficed to meet the demand. As greater depth is reached, the assumption is that still better coal shall be found. To a certainty, there is an abundance of the article in the colony to meet any demand that may arise for railway extension or manufacturing purposes.

Other Minerals.

Iron—chrome iron, brown and red hæmatite, and micaceous ores—are found in various parts of the colony; also bismuth, manganese, mercury ores, antimony ores, lead, silver, and other ores are continously coming to notice; and, as labour becomes more plentiful, no doubt they shall be worked. But, at present, the discoverers of such things quitely allow them to lay by until skill, capital, and labour are more plentiful.

There are various methods available for obtaining mineral lands, by lease and by purchase. There are no restrictions upon the working out of any mineral that a discoverer may see fit to follow. The cost of obtaining the land is low, and the regulations made bearing upon their working are for the purpose, far as it can be accomplished, of preventing monopolists from holding mineral lands for speculative purposes only.

Timbers of Queensland and Fibres.

The indigenous timbers are numerous, and several of them are of much value for house and ship building, and for the cabinet maker and the turner. Specimens of these valuable timbers are shown. The principal amongst them are of the family of eucalypti, which for strength, solidity, and durability, are very notable. The cedars of Queensland are peculiarly suitable for the cabinet makers and house decorators. They are easily worked, richly marked, light, and durable. The pines are useful for the same purposes and are exported largely, besides supplying very first-class timbers at low cost for house building purposes. The beech timbers are very easily worked, nicely marked, and durable. Further information on this subject is given in additions to Catalogue.

The fibres shown are from the vicinity of Brisbane mostly. The variety is extensive, and several, both indigenous and cultivated, are of undoubted mercantile value, and offer inducements for the enterprise of traders.

Manufactures.

From the rich abundance of raw material and the employment connected therewith, it may be surmised that manufactures have not made much headway. The policy of the country is for free trade; the duties from imports are more for the purpose of raising revenue than to advance towards protection. It is found that as a demand arrives, it is met by a local supply. Thus large foundries and iron works, supplying agricultural and mining machinery, have grown up at Brisbane, Maryborough, and other towns. Tanneries, several of them of large capacity, are at work near all the towns. A woolen factory has been established near Ipswich. Soap and candle factories, breweries, boot and shoe factories, confectionaries, coach, waggon, and cart builders, and many other callings grow steadily in number. They supply the local demand.

Occupations of the Population.

Subjoined are details of the occupations followed by colonists during the arranging of census statistics in 1876. Since then the population has increased steadily, but there is no material change in the average occupations:—

Census Districts.	Government Service.		Learned Professions.		Domestic Duties.		Personal Offices.		Commercial Businesses.		Pastoral.	
	M.	F.	M.	F.	M.	F.	M.	F.	M.	F.	M.	F.
Balonne ...	16	1	6	1	229	436	42	35	17	...	697	2
Blackall ...	22	...	3	1	32	60	20	16	9	...	741	4
Bowen ...	48	2	13	7	301	546	32	77	27	2	99	...
Brisbane ...	629	56	369	167	5,077	10,435	404	1,385	883	105	68	1
Bundaberg ...	23	1	5	4	368	650	28	54	20	...	37	1
Burnett ...	21	1	22	10	602	1,030	84	103	49	...	524	6
Burke ...	...	...	...	...	...	...	...	...	...	...	...	...
Caboolture ...	38	3	16	2	830	1,355	36	73	32	3	71	1
Cardwell ...	26	1	3	...	57	133	14	12	8	...	21	...
Charleville ...	19	...	1	...	72	145	29	11	5	...	649	5
Clermont ...	43	2	19	7	496	893	63	68	64	1	250	3
Cook ...	59	2	49	5	202	524	211	71	253	9	9	...
Cunnamulla ...	14	1	...	...	19	35	8	5	11	...	196	...
Dalby ...	40	3	23	14	499	1,007	44	89	62	2	87	2
D. Downs, Cent.	53	3	6	5	505	858	29	84	12	1	327	9
Ditto East	32	2	15	8	713	1,273	56	79	21	1	292	2
Ditto North	78	1	8	1	384	654	25	51	19	...	528	...
Ditto West	9	1	7	3	152	272	17	22	9	1	349	9
Drayton & Too.	117	11	83	47	2,203	3,626	131	325	147	18	111	27
Etheridge ...	16	...	3	...	48	84	25	12	20	2	27	...
Fassifern ...	6	2	9	3	401	745	4	36	9	...	74	1
Gilberton ...	3	...	...	...	3	10	2	1	1	...	5	...
Gladstone ...	34	5	1	7	315	549	25	60	21	1	127	5
Gympie ...	41	7	51	89	1,142	1,847	57	184	63	15	133	28
Ipswich ...	189	11	72	35	1,812	3,318	89	307	138	25	60	1
Kennedy North	70	1	39	4	593	1,330	159	111	98	2	217	5
Ditto South	5	...	...	...	26	73	10	13	3	...	202	1
Leichhardt ...	271	...	10	4	407	727	66	62	32	5	214	1
Logan ...	72	7	24	6	815	1,436	49	92	24	4	98	1
Mackay ...	35	4	18	6	469	921	74	148	60	2	123	...
Maranoa ...	35	...	26	10	432	742	74	117	40	4	669	7
Marathon ...	9	...	3	...	26	69	8	9	9	1	589	7
Maryborough	117	13	52	19	1,653	3,055	154	318	143	21	29	...
Moreton East	108	20	21	8	1,119	2,088	64	148	47	3	27	4
Ditto West	106	16	27	18	1,740	2,963	58	236	14	4	130	13
Oxley ...	169	25	49	9	1,437	2,692	62	174	72	7	55	3
Palmer ...	38	...	27	2	25	80	117	17	237	3	29	...
Peak Downs ...	29	1	8	2	108	194	58	52	16	...	446	...
Rockhampton	141	15	86	49	1,719	3,235	174	378	191	9	110	5
St. Lawrence...	21	1	11	4	268	492	48	79	17	2	201	5
Somerset ...	6	...	5	3	11	27	16	6	29	...	...	...
Springsure ...	15	...	3	4	133	274	52	51	23	2	288	...
Stanley ...	24	...	3	2	133	300	7	...	...	...	104	2
Stanthorpe ...	17	...	19	15	535	1,051	53	70	73	4	103	3
Tambo ...	12	1	7	...	32	52	22	13	7	...	113	...
Taroom	10	...	1	1	84	166	14	25	6	...	464	2
Tiaro ...	28	...	3	3	229	505	23	34	9	1	62	...
Townsville ...	51	...	31	12	452	962	163	147	103	5	37	2
Warrego ...	10	...	5	...	13	44	18	4	2	1	173	...
Warwick ...	44	10	27	16	857	1,646	91	166	94	7	68	1
Westwood ...	47	...	3	5	343	563	32	32	10	...	94	1
Wide Bay ...	26	1	15	2	213	424	33	37	8	...	132	1
TOTAL ...	3,092	231	1,307	620	30,334	56,596	3,174	5,699	3,269	273	10,259	171

Agricultural.		Carriers.		Trades.		Labourers		Public Burdens.		Unspecified.		Total.	
M.	F.	M.	F.	M.	F.	M.	F.	M.	F.	M.	F.	M.	F.
57	...	22	...	55	2	61	...	2	...	14	1	1,218	478
4	1	11	...	35	2	6	...	...	...	7	...	800	84
76	...	73	1	247	8	14	...	...	...	30	. 17	960	660
292	10	1,242	6	3,463	766	819	3	230	87	366	48	13,842	13,069
639	58	41	...	190	16	40	...	1	...	6	3	1,398	787
137	13	83	...	359	17	93	...	1	...	29	5	2,004	1,185
...	...	...	...	...	...	...	...	...	...	273	45	273	45
663	120	68	1	182	9	85	3	2	...	15	2	2,038	1,572
214	1	30	...	59	2	7	...	...	...	4	...	443	149
10	...	16	...	42	2	13	...	1	...	16	...	873	163
95	5	120	...	571	19	39	1	...	...	21	4	1,781	1,003
170	...	364	...	1,335	23	83	...	2	...	62	2	2,799	636
1	...	12	...	34	1	11	...	...	...	7	...	313	42
56	1	77	...	153	30	69	...	...	...	16	3	1,126	1,151
468	85	12	...	212	1	87	...	...	...	9	3	1,720	1,049
369	3	37	...	286	2	214	...	2	...	24	4	2,061	1,374
98	...	106	...	68	1	109	...	3	...	17	1	1,443	709
4	...	42	...	20	2	15	...	...	...	14	...	638	310
968	381	127	5	641	90	297	1	8	37	77	18	4,910	458
14	...	28	...	225	3	7	...	...	...	...	...	413	101
406	32	4	...	28	1	40	...	1	...	10	1	992	82
2	...	5	...	32	...	3	...	...	...	...	...	56	11
44	10	42	...	131	10	38	...	1	...	5	1	784	648
259	103	64	...	1,130	54	84	...	...	...	16	...	3,040	2,327
326	71	109	1	781	113	203	...	...	...	54	19	3,833	3,901
179	1	143	1	1,586	31	60	...	1	...	13	...	3,158	1,486
7	...	1	...	96	...	...	...	...	...	11	...	361	87
10	...	53	...	175	8	268	...	2	...	14	...	1,522	807
985	151	50	...	301	9	10	1	...	...	16	...	2,444	1,707
872	37	68	...	153	11	776	2	...	...	30	4	2,678	1,135
101	6	61	...	142	11	71	...	13	...	25	2	1,689	899
8	...	21	...	34	...	72	...	...	...	6	1	785	87
1,342	118	221	...	924	136	170	...	1	...	89	33	4,895	3,713
769	101	251	5	333	30	133	...	218	16	47	18	3,137	2,441
1,687	504	38	4	262	25	220	1	2	...	34	15	4,318	3,799
935	169	90	...	469	36	184	...	221	127	44	1	3,787	3,243
165	...	113	...	8,300	12	28	...	4	...	16	3	9,099	117
30	3	55	...	50	1	18	...	...	...	11	...	829	253
181	13	327	2	781	122	407	2	10	3	79	13	4,206	3,846
51	14	49	...	104	9	51	...	...	...	18	2	841	608
...	...	337	2	10	...	4	...	...	...	1	...	419	38
17	...	122	...	89	6	61	...	...	...	5	...	808	337
150	28	57	1	171	1	47	4	1	...	55	60	752	398
25	1	47	...	917	28	37	...	...	...	27	12	1,853	1,184
18	...	18	...	38	...	9	...	...	...	2	...	278	66
1	...	15	...	15	1	1	...	...	...	12	...	623	105
261	12	30	...	115	5	143	...	...	...	8	4	911	564
38	...	139	...	346	...	149	1	4	1	24	18	1,537	1,148
...	1	2	...	9	...	3	...	...	...	5	...	240	50
328	39	94	...	357	55	116	...	1	...	14	23	2,091	1,964
142	15	31	...	252	6	14	...	...	...	12	...	980	622
296	37	28	...	92	6	69	...	1	...	14	1	927	509
13,970	2,144	5,196	29	26,400	1,723	5,558	20	733	271	1,724	387	105,016	68,164

This population has grown as shown by the following figures :—

Population in 1846 (by census)	...	...	2,257
,,	on 31st December, 1861 ...	...	34,367
,,	on 1st Jan., 1864 (by census)	...	61,467
,,	on 2nd March, 1868 (by census) ...		99,312
,,'	on 1st Sept., 1871 (by census)	...	120,076
,,	on 30th June, 1873	...	...	139,668
,,	on 31st December, 1873 ...	...	146,690
,,	on 31st December, 1874 ...	...	163,517
,,	on 1st May, 1876 (by census)	...	173,283

As showing the increase of population by births, the following figures are explanatory :—

Year.	Number of Births Registered.	Number of Marriages Registered.	Number of Deaths Registered.	Increase to the Population from Excess of Births over Deaths.	Increase to Population from excess of Immigration over Emigration.	Estimated Population on Dec. 31.	Increase of Population on the previous year.
1875	6,706	1,487	4,104	2,602	15,169	181,238	17,771

Imports and Exports.

PORTS.		IMPORTS.		EXPORTS.	
		1875.	1876.	1875.	1876.
		£	£	£	£
Brisbane	... ...	2,204,849	2,051,894	1,589,346	1,757,679
Maryborough	... ...	213,110	149,014	251,047	246,055
Bundaberg	... ...	2,049	2,025	Nil	638
Gladstone	... ...	5,087	6,814	19,088	19,245
Rockhampton	... ...	299,419	322,102	529,398	600,915
St. Lawrence	... ...	29,854	33,752	3,953	4,821
Mackay	... ...	22,331	14,192	45,556	13,648
Bowen	... ...	23,680	22,208	18,340	12,899
Townsville	... ...	157,769	152,560	401,602	333,017
Cardwell	... ...	2,248	1,772	83,657	42,407
Trinity Bay	... ...	Nil	2,868	Nil	1,865
Cooktown	... ...	219,324	214,371	664,466	691,272
Somerset	... ...	Nil	2,028	Nil	14,264
Sweer's Island	... ...	14,622	8,270	1,878	1,534
Total seaward	...	3,194,342	2,983,870	3,608,331	3,740,259
Across the Border...	...	24,467	26,853	Nil	Nil
Live Stock overland	...	109,200	115,836	249,245	135,322
Totals	... ...	3,328,009	3,126,559	3,857,576	3,875,581

The nature of the exports are summarised in the annexed statement for 1875. The imports represent all that is used by an industrious well-to-do people, with the exception of food and the articles manufactured in the colony :—

					£
Antimony ore	...	...	...	88 tons ...	745
Arrowroot	...	...	...	122,329 lbs. ...	2,859
Barley	...	...	...	420 bushels	80
Black sand	...	...	...	15 tons ...	1,000
Beche-de-mere	...	...	...	1,523 cwt. ...	6,018
Bone and Bone dust	...	...	...	1,899 cwt. ...	693
Coals, Coke, and Fuel	...	...	...	2,795 tons ...	2,065
Copper ore	...	...	...	219 tons ...	5,714
Copper, smelted	...	...	...	1,291 tons ...	105,549
Cotton	...	...	...	314,454 lbs. ...	8,162
Cotton Seed	...	...	...	... ...	21
Fruit (green)	...	...	...	2,556 packages	2,749
Gold	...	...	...	391,515 ozs. ...	1,498,433
Hair	...	...	...	208 ...	940
Hides and Skins	...	...	...	... ...	80,386
Honey and Beeswax	...	...	...	... ...	271
Hoofs and Horns	...	...	...	... ...	783
Leather	...	...	...	... ...	5
Live stock, by sea and overland	...	...	...	... ...	261,785
Meat (fresh and preserved)	...	...	...	... ...	49,858
Ditto (essence of)	...	...	...	... ...	2,252
Molasses	...	...	...	1,061 cwt. ...	313
Plants	...	...	...	... ...	282
Rum	...	...	...	153,339 gallons	18,371
Seeds, &c.	...	...	...	... ...	30
Shell (Pearl)	...	...	...	... ...	799
Shell-fish (oysters)	...	...	...	... ...	2,622
Specimens of Natural History	...	...	...	... ...	438
Sugar	...	...	...	2,864 tons ...	70,007
Tallow	...	...	...	1,385 tons ...	43,001
Timber	...	...	...	... ...	26,884
Tin ore	...	...	...	77,709 cwt. ...	190.671
Tin (smelted)	...	...	...	11,788 cwt. ...	47,208
Turtle (preserved)	...	...	...	... ...	197
Wool	...	...	...	20,145,914 lbs. ...	1,366,030

Climate of Queensland.

As will be surmised from the foregoing, the climate that enables a handful of people to export so much in addition to supporting themselves is a favourable one. The climate of Queensland well deserves that reputation. The summer temperature is hot, but not to the extent that might be judged by the latitude and longitude of the country, or by thermometer indications. The absolute heat is tempered by breezes peculiar to the country, and which allow of out-door labour, agricultural, pastoral, mining, travelling, and all in-door business being transacted without undue exhaustion or injury to health, at all times of the year, and in all parts of the country. This summer season extends from August through to March.

The winter season, from March to August, is delightful. In the far western and elevated districts very decided frost is experienced at night during that season, and in the country frost is also felt, but not so heavily. It is during this winter season that the wheat and similar crops come to such perfection.

System of Government.

Queensland is governed after the manner of Government in Great Britain; but, with the exception of appointing the Governor, which is an Imperial privilege, the making of laws and the whole of the administration, including the levying, collection, and expenditure of revenue, are attended to by the colonists, without any interference whatever. They pay nothing to the mother country; there are no military in Queensland; the colonists govern themselves. There are two Houses of Legislature—the Council and the Assembly. To the latter the members are elected by the general public—the suffrage being, practically, universal. The Upper House is nominated by the Government; the members of the Upper House hold their seats for life. The Government or Executive for the time being must, on all essential questions, have a majority of the elective Chamber as their supporters. Failing this, they resign, and the stronger party assume the reigns of power. In Queensland the system works well; the country has been fortunate in her representative men, and in the various Governments that have been in power.

Queensland Tariff.

The articles upon which duties are levied, and the amounts levied, are :—

Acids, 4s. per cwt.
Arrowroot, 2d. per lb.
Barley, 6d. per bushel.
Bacon and Hams, 2d. per lb.
Beer (in bottle), 1s. for six reputed quart bottles.
Ditto, 1s. for twelve reputed pint bottles
Beer (in wood), 9d. per gallon.
Biscuits, 2d. per lb.
Blue, 1d. per lb.
Boats, 2s. 6d. per foot overall.
Brandy, 12s. per gallon.
Bran and Pollard, 2d. per bushel.
Butter, 2d. per lb.
Candles, 2d. per lb.
Castor Oil (in bottle), 1s. per dozen pints; and in same proportion for larger or smaller quantities.
Castor Oil, 6d. per gallon.
Cement, 2s. per barrel.
Cider and Perry (in bottle), 1s. for six reputed quart bottles.
Ditto, 1s. for twelve reputed pint bottles.

Ditto (in wood), 9d. per gallon.
Cigars, 5s. per lb.
Cheese, 2d. per lb.
Chicory, 4d. per lb.
Coals, 1s. 6d. per ton.
Cocoa and Chocolate, 4d. per lb.
Cocoa—Raw, 2d. per lb.
Corrugated Iron, 2s. per cwt.
Coffee—Roasted, 6d. per lb.
Ditto—Raw, 4d. per lb.
Confectionery and Succades, 2d. per lb.
Cordials, 10s. per gallon.
Cordage and Rope, 4s. per cwt.
Cornflour, 1d. per lb.
Doors, 2s. 6d. each.
Dried Fruits, 2d. per lb.
Fish—Pickled and salted (in casks), 5s. per cwt.
Ditto, dried, 5s. per cwt.
Ditto, preserved (not salted), 2s. per dozen lbs., and in same proportion for larger or smaller contents
Fruits (bottled or in tins), 1s. per dozen pints or lbs.

Galvanized Iron, 2s. per cwt.
Geneva, 10s. per gallon.
Ginger, 2d. per lb.
Glue, 2d. per lb.
Gunpowder, 1d. per lb.
Hay and Chaff, 10s. per ton.
Honey, 2d. per lb.
Hops, 2d. per lb.
Iron Castings, for building purposes, 2s. per cwt.
s, 8s. each.
Salad Oil, 1s. per dozen pints, and in same proportion for larger or smaller contents.
Saltpetre, 4s. per cwt.
Sarsaparilla—containing more than 25 per cent. of alcohol of specific gravity of ·825 at the temperature of 60 degrees Fahrenheit's thermometer, 10s. per gallon.
Sarsaparilla—not containing more than 25 per cent. of alcohol, 4s. per gallon.
Sashes, 2s. 6d. per pair.
Shot, 2s. per cwt.
Screws, 2s. per cwt.
Snuff, 2s. 6d. per lb.
Soap—not including toilet soap, 5s. per cwt.
Soda and Soda Crystals, 1s. per cwt.
Spices, 2d. per lb.
Spirits—Perfumed, 10s. per gallon.
Ditto—All other, 10s. per gallon.
Spruce and other Beer—in glass, 1s. per gallon.
Ditto—in wood, 9d. per gallon.
Starch, 1d. per lb.
Sugar—Refined, 6s. 8d. per cwt.
Ditto—Raw, 5s. per cwt.
Iron Wire, 2s. per cwt.
Jams and Jellies, 1s. per dozen reputed lbs., and in same proportion for larger or smaller contents
Lead—Red and White, 2s. per cwt.

Leather—2d. per lb.
Maccaroni, 1d. per lb.
Maize, 6d. per bushel.
Maizena, 1d. per lb.
Maizemeal, 1d. per lb.
Malt, 6d. per bushel.
Methylated Spirits, 5s. per gallon.
Molasses, 3s. 4d. per cwt.
Mustard, 2d. per lb.
Nails, 2s. per cwt.
Nuts—all sorts, except cocoanuts—2d. per lb.
Oatmeal, 40s. per ton.
Old Tom, 10s. per gallon.
Oils, Mineral, &c., 6d. per gallon.
Onions, 10s. per ton.
Opium, 20s. per lb.
Oats, 6d. per bushel.
Paints—Wet and dry, 2s. per cwt.
Pepper, 2d. per lb.
Pickles, 1s. per dozen pints, and in same proportion for larger or smaller contents.
Potatoes, 10s. per ton.
Preserved Meat—not salted, 2s. per dozen lbs., and in same proportion for larger or smaller contents.
Rice, 1d. per lb.
Rum—Foreign, 10s. per gallon.
Sauces, 1s. per dozen pints, and in same proportion for larger or smaller contents.
Sago, 1d. per lb.
Tapioca, 1d. per lb.
Tea, 6d. per lb.
Tobacco, 2s. 6d. per lb.
Turpentine, 6d. per gallon.
Twine, 1d. per lb.
Vermicelli, 1d. per lb.
Vinegar—in wood, 9d. per gallon.
Ditto—in bottle, 1s. per gallon.
Wheat, 6d. per bushel.
Whisky, 10s. per gallon.
Wine, not containing more than 25 per cent. alcohol, 6s. per gallon.

Ad valorem duties to the extent of five per cent., or a duty of five pounds has to be paid for every £100 of the value of all articles imported which are not mentioned in the foregoing schedule, or in the annexed list of articles exempted from duty. The articles exempted or admitted free from all duty are :—

Anchors.
Animals, alive.
Boiler plates.
Books, printed.
Chain cables, over ⅜ of an inch in diameter.

Copper coin.
  „ sheet, plain.
Curiosities—antique.
Flax, New Zealand.
Flour.
Gold coin.

Ditto, unmanufactured.
Garden seeds.
  Ditto produce.
  Ditto bulbs.
  Ditto trees.
  Ditto shrubs.
Green fruit.
Iron ore.
Ditto, plain sheet, not including galvanized.
Ditto, pig.
Ditto, bar.
Ditto, rod.
Ditto, scrap.
Ditto, hoop.
Lead, pig.
Ditto, sheet.
Manure.

Machinery, agricultural.
  Ditto   manufacturing.
  Ditto   mining.
  Ditto   pastoral purposes.
  Ditto   sawing.
  Ditto   sewing.
  Ditto   steam engine and boilers.
Muntz metal.

Newspapers— printed.

Naval and military stores, imported for the service of the Colonial Governments, or for the use of Her Majesty's land or sea forces; and wines and spirits for the use of His Excellency the Governor, or, for naval and military officers employed on actual naval or military service and on full pay.

Outside packages, in which goods are ordinarily imported, and which are of no commercial value except as covering for goods.

Passengers' cabin furniture and baggage, and passengers' personal effects (not including vehicles, musical instruments, glassware, chinaware, silver and gold plate, and plated goods, and furniture other than cabin furniture), which are imported with and by passengers *bona fide* for their own personal use, and not imported for the purpose of sale.

Quicksilver.
Salt.
Specimens, natural history.
Silver coin.
Ditto unmanufactured.
Tin plates.
Ditto block.
Zinc.

Religious and Social Affairs.

There is no political or State interference whatever with religious affairs. They are entirely under the control of those concerned; and to the credit of colonists be it said that, while all denominations, creeds, sects and beliefs are, or may be represented, there is no disposition amongst the people to show hostility or to carp at the creed of their neighbours.

Education is under the control of the State, the chief of the Education Department being a member of the Government for the time being. Education is free, and in the towns and more thickly settled districts it reaches all parties. In the thinly settled districts this is not easily accomplished; but it is attempted by appointing irregular teachers.

The plan that has worked so well with the churches is being followed in the schools. There is no denominational interference on the part of the State. All creeds and phases of religious belief are upon the same footing. Respect for the laws of God and man is taught, and the ground work of a sound English education given.

The school teachers of Queensland are a carefully selected body, and do their work in a manner that is satisfactory to the public. There is no interference with their religious belief, nor are they allowed to proselytise in any form whatever. The position of teacher is obtained by examination in the colony. Certificates of competency from other known educational institutions having their due weight in securing appointments. The salaries paid to teachers range from £100 to £200 per annum for males, and £80 to £170 for females.

The Press is fully represented in Queensland. In Brisbane are one daily morning and one evening journal, and there are five weekly papers and two or three monthlies. Ipswich has two journals; Rockhampton, three; Maryborough, two; Toowoomba, two; Warwick, two; Dalby, one; Stanthorpe, one; Roma, one; Gympie, one; Bundaberg and Mount Perry, two; Bowen, one; Mackay, two; Townsville, two; Cooktown, two; Peak Downs, two; and there is a journal published in each of the established mining townships.

Emigration to Queensland.

The colony has ever been desirous of introducing industrious people from various parts of the world. Men of capital find their way to Queensland of their own accord. There is no lack of capital in the colony, nor has capital to go begging for investment. The opening up of new country for grazing and farming, new townships, new goldfields, new manufactures of raw material found in the colony, and in order to supply the always increasing demands of a prosperous, pushing people, afford abundant openings for capital and enterprise.

The demand for working men and women of all kinds is steady. Industrious people can, at all times, depend upon obtaining employment of some kind; and, as a rule, it has proved to be the best course to accept, at the commencement, such employment as offers.

Mechanics and tradesmen, especially those connected with the building trades, are in continuous demand, and careful skilful men are soon able to start on their own account. Subjoined is a tabular statement of the average wages paid for the leading occupations followed. The rate does not fluctuate much :—

Trade or Occupation.	Per Annum with Rations.*	Per Week with Rations.	Per Day without Rations.	Per Month without Rations.	General Remarks.
Agricultural Labourers—					
Married	£55 to £60	...	...	...	...
Single	£40 to £50	...	...	...	...
Boys, 12 to 16	...	10s. to 12s.	...	...	...
Butchers	...	25s. to 30s.	...	...	...
Bookbinders	...	...	...	...	£3 per week.
Bakers	£50 to £60	...	...	...	...
Brickmakers	...	...	7s. or 16s. per 1,000	...	...
Bricklayers	...	...	10s. 8 hours	...	...
Bricklayers' Labourers	...	...	6s. to 7s. 6d.	...	...
Blacksmiths	...	...	8s. to 9s. 8 hours	...	...
Bullock Drivers... ...	£50	...	...	...	...
Bush Carpenters ...	£60	...	...	...	...
Compositors	...	...	...	...	1s. and 13d. per 1,000 ens
Carters	...	...	5s. to 6s.	...	...
Carpenters	...	...	8s. to 10s.	...	...
Joiners	...	...	8s. to 9s.	...	...
Cabinet Makers... ...	...	...	8s. to 9s.	...	...
Coachmen and Grooms	£45 to £50	...	...	...	...
Cooks—					
Male	£50	...	...	...	...
Female	£35 to £40	...	...	...	...
Coopers	...	...	10s.	...	...
Engineers	...	...	...	£12 to £16	...
Farm Labourers ...	£40 to £50	...	...	...	...
Glaziers and Painters ...	...	...	9s.	...	...
Gardeners	£50	...	...	...	...
Saddlers	...	...	8s. to 10s.	...	...
Hutkeepers	£30 to £35	...	...	...	...
Iron Founders	...	...	12s.	...	...
Masons	...	...	10s. to 12s.	...	...
Millwrights	...	...	...	£12 to £15	...
Ostlers	£45	...	...	...	...
Ploughmen	£50 to £55	...	...	...	...
Plasterers	...	...	10s.	...	...
Plumbers	...	...	10s.	...	...
Quarrymen	...	...	7s. 6d. to 9s.	...	...
Shoeing Smiths	...	...	10s. to 12s.	...	...
Storemen	...	...	...	...	£50 to £100 per annum
Sawyers	£60	...	...	...	...
Shoemakers	...	...	8s. to 10s.	...	...
Shipwrights	...	...	10s.	...	...
Shepherds	£40 to £45	...	...	...	...
Stone Dressers	...	...	10s. to 12s.	...	...
Tailors	...	...	10s.	...	...
Wheelwrights	...	...	10s. to 12s.	...	...
Whitesmiths	...	...	10s.	...	...

FEMALES.

Trade or Occupation.	Per Annum with Rations.*	Per Week with Rations.	Per Day without Rations.	Per Month without Rations.	General Remarks.
Cooks	£30 to £35	...	...	...	...
Cooks and Laundresses	£30 to £40	...	...	...	...
General Servants ...	£30 to £35	...	...	...	...
Housemaids	£24 to £26	...	...	...	...
Housekeepers	£35 to £40	...	...	...	...
Nurses	£30	...	...	...	...
Nursemaids	£18 to £20	...	...	...	...
Needlewomen	...	...	...	...	2s. to 2s. 6d. per day with bd.
Dressmakers	...	...	...	...	2s. 6d. to 3s. per day with bd.
Waitresses	£30 to £35	...	...	...	...
Ladies' Maids	£30 to £35	...	...	...	...
Laundresses	£26 to £30	...	...	...	...

* Rations are generally 8 lbs. of flour, 17 lbs. beef, 2 lbs. sugar, ¼ lb. tea weekly, or board, as may be agreed.

In order to supply the continuous demand for labour, free and assisted passages are given to the colony to persons considered to be suitable. A department, under the care of an Agent-General for Queensland, is maintained in London for the purpose of sending emigrants forward. The office of this department is at 32 Charing Cross, and enquires made there personally or by letter to the Agent-General, Arthur Macalister, Esquire, elicits all the information desired.

The class of persons most in demand at present are female domestic servants, and labourers experienced in farm, out-door, and railway work. As extensive railway works are in contemplation, there will be an active demand for the latter class for some years to come. To all the classes mentioned, when eligible in point of health and character, free passages are granted. Forms of application can be had that give all necessary information.

Assisted passages are granted to mechanics, tradesmen, and others, who may be considered suitable for colonists. The rates charged are :—

> For males from 1 year old to 12 years £2; between 12 and 40, £4; above 40, £6.
> For females from 1 year old to 12 years £1; between 12 and 40, £2; above 40, £6.

Great care is exercised in selecting, officering, and provisioning ships that carry passengers to Queensland. The whole is directly under the care of the Agent-General. These ships sail from London, Glasgow, and other ports in Britain for Brisbane, Rockhampton, and other Queensland ports. One or two vessels sail for the colony each month. This traffic has been going on for many years, and has been very successful all along. Casualties have seldom occurred. The voyage occupies from 90 to 120 days, and is usually pleasant throughout. On the voyage the passengers are supplied with an abundance of all necessaries, and they arrive in full health and excellent condition.

There are depôts in the colony for the reception of new arrivals, where they are provided with food and lodging without charge until they find employment. This seldom takes much time. The usual occurrence is that one cargo of immigrants have found employment before the next arrives.

In the colony, life moves along pretty much after the English model. The colonists work hard and mind their own business. The prevailing disposition is to allow each man and woman to follow their own affairs in the way each likes best. In the towns social, benevolent, patriotic, and other societies prevail, and carry on their affairs without any molestation whatever.

Annexed is a table of distances between the principal towns and places of note connected with them :—

BRISBANE

			Miles.
To Sandgate	... ...	E.	12
„ Ipswich	... ...	W.	25
„ Maryborough	...	N.	200
„ Gladstone (Port Curtis)	... ...	N.	300
„ Rockhampton	...	N.	400
„ St. Lawrence (Broad Sound)	...	N.	500
„ Mackay (Port)	...	N.	600
„ Bowen (Port Denison)		N.	700
„ Townsville (Cleveland Bay)	... ...	N.	850
„ Cardwell (Rockingham Bay)	...	N.	950
„ Somerset (Torres Straits)		N.	1,700

BRISBANE

To Cleveland	... ...	S.	25
„ Caboolture	... ...	N.	30
„ Nerang Creek	...	S.	55
„ Toowoomba	...	W.	105
„ Warwick	...	S.W.	105
„ Stanthorpe	...	S.W.	145
„ Neusa Creek	...	N.	110
„ Gympie	... ...	N.	125
„ Dalby	... ...	W.N.W.	130
„ Gayndah	... ...	N.	200
„ Condamine	...	N.W.	200
„ Goodiwindi (border)		W.S.W.	280
„ Roma	... ...	W.	290
„ Surat	... ...	W.	300
„ Taroom (Dawson river)		N.W.	320
„ Mitchell Downs	...	W.	340
„ St. George (Balonne)		W.	400
„ Curriwillinghi (border)	... ...	W.S.W.	400
„ Charleville	... ...	W.	470
„ Springsure	... ...	N.W.	530
„ Peak Downs	...	N.N.W.	600
„ Tambo (Barcoo)	...	N.W.	620
„ Nebo	...	N.N.W.	650
„ Alice Downs	...	N.W.	700
„ Ravenswood	...	N.N.W.	750
„ Cooper's Creek	...	W.	850
„ Bowen Downs	...	N.W.	850
„ Marathon	...	N.W.	1,050
„ Burke Town (Gulf)		N.W.	1,450

ROCKHAMPTON

To Westwood	... ...	S.W.	30
„ Mont Wheeler Mines		N.E.	30
„ Morinish	... ...	N.	30
„ Princhester	...	N.	50
„ Marlborough	...	N.	60
„ Gladstone	...	S.E.	80
„ Canal Creek	...		120
„ Broad Sound	...	N.	130
„ Taroom	... ...	S.	250

ROMA

			Miles.
To Surat	... ...	S.	50
„ Mitchell Downs	...	W.	54
„ Condamine	...	E.	90
„ Taroom	... ...	N.	120

STANTHORPE

To N. S. W. (Border)	...	S.	12

BUNDABERG

To Mount Perry	...	W.	60

ST. GEORGE

To Surat	... ...	N.	90
„ Curriwillinghi (Border)		S.	100
„ Dalby	... ...	E.	270

ST. LAWRENCE
(Broad Sound)

To Nebo	... ...	N.W.	110

MACKAY

To Nebo	... ...	N.W.	60
„ St. Lawrence	...	S.E.	100

TOWNSVILLE

To Dalrymple	... ...	W.	75
„ Lower Herbert	...	N.	95
„ Charters Towers	...	W.	100
„ Bowen	... ...	S.E.	100
„ Valley of Lagoons	...	N.W.	230

CARDWELL.
(Rockingham Bay)

To Lower Herbert	...	S.W.	45
„ Valley of Lagoons	...	W.	95
„ Townsville	...	S.E.	120
„ Lyndhurst	...	W.	200
„ Georgetown	...	W.	230
„ Gulf of Carpentaria		W.	350

RAVENSWOOD

To Dalrymple	... ...	N.W.	80
„ Townsville	... ...	N.E.	115

GYMPIE

To Imbil Diggings	...	S.	25
„ Kilkivan	...	N.W.	40
„ Maryborough	...	N.E.	55

SPRINGSURE

To Albinia Downs	...	W.	50
„ Gainsford (Dawson)		E.	115
„ Clermont	... ...	N.	135

CLERMONT

			Miles.
To Copperfield...	...	s.	4
„ Nebo	...	N.E.	130
„ Beauford ...	...	s.w.	140
„ Broad Sound	...	E.	150
„ Gainsford ...	...	s.E.	180
„ The Thompson	...	w.	230

GLADSTONE

To Cania Diggings	...	s.	110
„ Banana ...	...	N.w.	130

GAYNDAH.

To Mount Perry	...	w.	45
„ Maryborough	...	E.	85
„ Nanango ...	...	s.	100
„ Dalby ...	...	s.w.	140
„ Banana ...	...	N.	150
„ Taroom ...	...	N.w.	160

DALRYMPLE (Burdekin River)

To Cape River ...	...	w.	80
„ Richmond Downs ...	w.	270
„ George Town	...	N.w.	340

MARYBOROUGH.

To Bundaberg (Port) ...	N.	80

TOOWOOMBA

To Drayton	...	w.	4
„ Dalby	...	N.w.	50
„ Allora	...	s.	50
„ Warwick	...	s.	65

WARWICK

To Talgai	...	N.w.	30
„ Stanthorpe Tin Mines	s.w.	40
„ Leyburn	...	N.w.	42

BOWEN
(Port Denison)

			Miles.
To Mount Dryander	...	s.E.	40
„ Mount McConnell	...	w.	120
„ Ravenswood	...	w.	130
„ Mackay	...	s.E.	90
„ Belyando Crossing	...	s.w.	150
„ Dalrymple	...	w.	160
„ Nebo	...	s.	170
„ Clermont	...	s.s.w.	260
„ Bowen Downs	...	w.	350

BOWEN DOWNS

To Hughenden ...	...	N.	145
„ Blackall (Alice Downs)	...	s.	165

BLACKALL
(Barcoo R.)

To Springsure	...	E.	240
„ Marathon (Flinders)	N.	350

NORMANTOWN

To Georgetown ...	...	E.	250

BURKETOWN
(Gulf Carpentaria)

To Normantown	...	E.	120
„ Gilbertown	...	E.	300
„ Carpentaria Downs ...	E.	350
„ Richmond Downs	...	s.E.	350
„ Hughenden	...	s.E.	480
„ Bowen Downs	...	s.	600
„ Alice Downs (Barcoo)	s.E.	750
„ Fort Bourke (N.S.W.)	s.	1,350

Shipping.
SIGNALS IN USE AT QUEENSLAND PORTS.

PILOT—Union Jack at the fore.

PILOT BOAT—White and red flag, horizontal.

CUSTOMS—Union Jack at the peak.

WATER POLICE (Day Signal)—Ensign at the main.

WATER POLICE (Night Signal)—Gun to be fired, and a bright light hoisted at the peak and the mizen.

STEAMBOAT—Rendezvous flag at the peak or mizen.

GUNPOWDER ON BOARD—Union Jack at the main.

HEALTH OFFICER—Blue flag at the main.

MAILS ON BOARD—White flag at the fore, to be kept flying until the mails are delivered.

ENGLISH MAILS—Ensign at the fore.

EXEMPTION (Day Signal)—White flag at the main.

EXEMPTION (Night Signal)—Two bright lights, vertical, hoisted at a distance of six feet between each lantern, in some conspicuous part of the vessel.

GOVERNMENT IMMIGRANTS ON BOARD—Ensign at the mizen.

QUARANTINE—Yellow flag at the main.

HARBOUR AND LIGHT DUES LEVIED IN QUEENSLAND.

LIGHT DUES.

	Inwards.	Outwards.
Foreign-going vessels	3d. per ton ...	3d per ton.
Intercolonial trade vessels ...	1½d. „ ...	1½d. „
Coasting vessels	1d. „ ...	1d. „

Additional charges to foreign vessels for any two coast lights passed—1d. per ton each.

Additional charges to intercolonial vessels for any two coast lights passed—½d. per ton each.

Additional charges to coasters for any two coast lights passed—¼d. per ton each.

Vessels engaged in the whaling trade, vessels in ballast, and vessels compelled by stress of weather to enter or put back into any port of the colony, are exempt from the payment of light dues.

Vessels of fifteen tons and upwards plying for hire or trading within any port of the colony, where one or more harbour lights are maintained, pay to the Collector or other chief officer of Customs at such port, towards the maintenance of the light or lights within such port, an annual rate of one shilling per ton; and such rate is to be paid on the 1st day of January in each year.

At any ports where no coast light is exhibited, harbour lights are paid for by sea-going vessels at the rate proportioned to their cost of maintenance—the scale being fixed by the Marine Board.

PILOTAGE RATES.

On arrival from sea at, and departure to sea from, the undermentioned ports and anchorages :—

Anchorages.	Rate per ton. s. d.	Minimum. £ s. d.
Brisbane River, above Bar		
Fitzroy River, above Rocky Point		
Mary River, above North Head	0 6	3 0
Norman and Albert Rivers		
Brisbane Roads, or above Pilot Station, Moreton Bay; Broad Mount or above the Light-ship, Keppel Bay; Burnett River, above lower anchorage		
White Cliffs, Great Sandy Island Strait, or above that anchorage	0 5	2 0 0
Port Curtis, above Observatory Point		
Broad Sound, above Basin		
Sweer's Island		
Pilot Station, Moreton Island		
Sea Hill, Keppel Bay		
Observatory Point, Port Curtis		
Burnett Mouth		
Baffle Creek		
Basin, Broad Sound	0 4	1 10 0
Pioneer River		
Port Denison		
Cleveland Bay		
Port Hinchinbrook		
Port Douglas, Island Point		
Endeavour River		

Vessels in ballast, and vessels returning to port through stress of weather, pay half above rates.

Vessels clearing out for more than one port, pay full rates at first and half rates at all other ports in original clearance.

Coasters under 50 tons, when not employing a pilot, are exempt from above rates.

Every vessel not exempt from pilotage, and every vessel employing the services of a pilot for berthing or removal, or on board of which the harbor master or his deputy proceeds for the purpose of berthing or removal (such removal not being for the purpose of leaving the port) pays the following dues :—

TONNAGE.	Under 3 miles.	3 to 10 miles.	10 to 20 miles.	20 to 30 miles.	Upwards of 30 miles.
	£ s.	£ s.	£ s.	£ s.	£ s.
Every vessel under 100 tons ...	0 10	0 15	1 0	1 5	1 10
„ 100 to 200 „ ...	1 0	1 5	1 10	1 15	2 0
„ 200 „ 300 „ ...	1 5	1 11	1 17	2 3	2 10
„ 300 „ 400 „ ...	1 10	1 17	2 5	2 12	3 0
„ 400 „ 500 „ ...	1 15	2 4	2 12	3 1	3 10
„ 500 „ 600 „ ...	2 0	2 10	3 0	3 10	4 0
„ 600 „ 700 „ ...	2 5	2 16	3 7	3 19	4 10
„ 700 „ 800 „ ...	2 10	3 2	3 15	4 7	5 0
„ 800 „ 900 „ ...	2 15	3 9	4 2	4 16	5 10
„ 900 „ 1000 „ ...	3 0	3 15	4 10	5 5	6 0
„ 1000 „ 1200 „ ...	3 5	4 3	5 1	6 0	7 0
„ 1200 „ 1500 „ ...	3 10	4 13	5 16	7 0	8 0
„ 1500 „ 2000 „ ...	4 0	5 10	7 0	8 10	10 0
„ over 2000 „ ...	5 0	6 15	8 10	10 5	12 0

Every decked vessel trading between any port, pays once in the month of January and once in the month of July in each year the highest pilotage rate per ton chargeable in respect of such port (the minimum payment being one pound).

Every coaster under 50 tons, and every vessel commanded by a master holding from the Marine Board of Queensland a certificate of exemption from pilotage for any port, pays once in every six months in which she enters the port the highest pilotage rate payable in respect of any anchorage within such port, and makes such payment upon the first occasion after the 1st of January and the 1st of July respectively that such vessel enters such port without employing a pilot. Such payment in the aggregate not to exceed two shillings per ton in any such six months.

No such coaster or vessel is required to pay such rates at more than two ports upon her first voyage, and if upon her first voyage during the six months she enters more than two ports, she pays the said rates for all ports after the first two upon the next occasion of her entering them respectively.

All rates and dues are paid to the Chief Officer of Customs at the port where the same are levied.

Vessels in the service of, or belonging to Her Majesty are exempt from all rates and dues.

MARINE BOARD OF QUEENSLAND.   £ s. d.

For every certificate granted by the Board to the owner of any steam vessel—

Where the tonnage of such vessel does not exceed 100 tons, a sum not exceeding 1 0 0

Where such tonnage exceeds 100 tons, and does not exceed 300 tons, a sum not exceeding 2 0 0

Where such tonnage exceeds 300 tons, a sum not exceeding ... 3 0 0

No certificate to be in force more than six months.

CERTIFICATES AND LICENSES.	£	s.	d.
Certificate of exemption ...	5	0	0
Certificate of competency to a master of a colonial trade vessel	5	0	0
Ditto to a master of a coasting vessel only	2	10	0
License to a pilot ...	2	2	0
License to a ballast boat ...	2	2	0
License to a gunpowder boat	2	2	0
License for oyster layings ...	5	0	0
License for men employed on ditto, each	0	10	0
License for boat of three tons	1	0	0
For every additional ton ...	0	10	0

SHIPPING MASTERS—BRISBANE, MARYBOROUGH, PORT CURTIS, ROCKHAMPTON, BROAD SOUND, PIONEER RIVER, PORT DENISON, CLEVELAND BAY, PORT HINCHINBROOK, AND ENDEAVOUR RIVER.

	£	s.	d.
Engagement of seamen, each	0	2	0
Discharge of seamen, each	0	2	0
Certificates of permission to be employed, each	0	5	0
On registering lodging-house license	0	5	0
Foreign-going ship's articles	0	5	0
Colonial ditto	0	2	6
Advance notes	0	0	6
Account of wages ...	0	0	3
Special clearance form	0	0	6

Lighthouses on the Queensland Coast.

The following is a brief description of the various lighthouses on the coast of Queensland, prepared by Captain Heath, in charge of that department :—

Name of Lighthouse or Lightship.	Description of Structure.	Nature of the Light.
Brisbane Bar ...	Lightship...	White Dioptric, fixed.
Cape Moreton ...	Stone Lighthouse	1st order, Catoptric, revolving at intervals of one minute.
Comboyuro Point ...	Wooden Lighthouse	4th order, Holophotal, showing red to seaward.
Cowan Cowan Point ...	ditto	4th order, Holophotal, fixed white and red.
Yellow Patch ...	ditto	5th order, white fixed, being altered to 4th order, white and red.
Leading Lights, Moreton Bay	Three pile lights and two beacon lights	One white, one green, one red, on piles, and one white and one red beacon, fixed.
Leading Lights, Brisbane River	Six beacon lights...	Three white, three red, fixed.
Leading Lights, Lytton	Wooden ...	One white, fixed.
Wide Bay Leading Lights	Two beacon lights	Two white, fixed.
Cleveland Point ...	Wooden Lighthouse	Fixed white.
Woody Island ...	Two wooden ditto	Two 4th order Dioptric Holophotal, condensing white and red.
Sandy Cape ...	Iron Lighthouse ...	1st order, Dioptric, revolving, white with glass reflecting mirrors.

LIGHTHOUSES ON THE QUEENSLAND COAST—*continued.*

Name of Lighthouse or Lightship.	Description of Structure.	Nature of the Light.
Lady Elliot's Island ...	Wooden Lighthouse sheathed with galvanised iron plates	4th order, Dioptric Holophotal, revolving flashes at intervals of thirty seconds.
Burnett Heads... ...	Wooden Lighthouse	5th order, Catoptric, fixed.
Burnett River Leading Lights	Beacon	Three white and one red, fixed, on beacons.
Bustard Head	Iron Lighthouse ...	2nd order, Dioptric, white and red, fixed, varied by flashes.
Bustard Head Screened Light, Outer Rock	Wooden Lighthouse	5th order, white, fixed.
Gatcombe Head ...	ditto ...	4th order, Dioptric, fixed, white and red.
Ditto ⎰Holophoto	ditto on shore	6th order, Holophote, fixed, white.
Oyster Rock ⎱Apparent Light	Iron on rock ...	Apparent.
Cape Capricorn ...	Iron Lighthouse ...	3rd order, Dioptric, revolving at intervals of one minute.
Sea Hill, Curtis Island	Wooden framework ⎱10 ft.	Leading light for rounding Timandra Bank.
Pilot Station, ditto ...	ditto	ditto ditto.
Keppel Bay	Lightship... ...	Dioptric, lense, white, fixed.
Upper Flats, Fitzroy River	ditto	Red, fixed; also tidal signals.
Upper Flats, Leading Lights	Beacons	Two white, fixed.
Pioneer River, Leading Lights	ditto	Eight leading lights, white, fixed.
Flat-top Island... ...	Wooden tower sheathed with galvanised iron plates	Temporary light, to be replaced by a 4th order, fixed, white.
North Head, Port Denison	Wooden Lighthouse	5th order, Dioptric, white and red.
Jetty Light, Port Denison	ditto ...	Red, fixed.
Cleveland Bay Leading Light	Beacons	Leading lights, two white and one red.
Cairns, Trinity Bay, Leading Light	ditto ...	ditto ditto.
Cape Bowling Green ...	Iron Lighthouse ...	3rd order, revolving every minute, white.
No. VI. Claremont Island	Lightship... ...	Dioptric, white, fixed.
Piper Island	ditto ...	ditto.
Torres Straits	ditto ...	ditto.
North Reef, Capricorn Group	Wooden Lighthouse sheathed with galvanised iron plates, 45 feet high	2nd order, two minutes, fixed, followed by two flashes at intervals of one minute.
Low Islands, Trinity Bay	ditto ditto	3rd order, one minute revolutions.

The Exhibits sent from Queensland.

These, although fewer in number than could be desired, afford a fair idea of the products of the colony. The native weapons are sent as matters of curiosity only, neither the natives nor their weapons being of much moment to the colonists. The kangaroo and other skins sent, could be obtained in any desired numbers. The fibres are largely available by cultivation. The sugars, grains, and other farm products are of the usual quality. The minerals are such as are produced every day, and of which no estimate can be made of the quantity available.

The pictures, of which the collection is full and varied, give a fair idea of colonial life, and the nature of the country, many of the groupings supplied in detailed illustration what is but briefly referred to in the foregoing descriptions of life as it is in Queensland.

LIST OF EXHIBITS AND EXHIBITORS.

MINERALS.

Nos.

1. GOLD SPECIMENS—
   One specimen of Palmer River gold, 3 ozs. 11 dwts. Collection of specimens from No. 4, South Caledonian Reef. Collection of specimens from Alma Reef. Collection of specimens from New Zealand Prospect Claim. One specimen from Warren Hastings Reef. } Goldfield Gympie
   Exhibited by Queensland Government.

2. GOLD SPECIMENS—
   44 in number. Gold shown in various matrices.
   Exhibited by N. Bartley, Brisbane.

3. COLLECTION OF ORES—
   Mount Perry Mines Copper District. 1. Antimony ; 2, 3, 4, 5, Galena (silver bearing) ; 6, Red Oxide of Copper, with Green Carbonate of Copper; 7, 8, 9, 10, Red Oxide of Copper Chalcotrichite ; 11, 12, Blue Carbonate of Copper; 13, Grey Copper Ore ; 14, Copper Pyrites ; 15, 16, 17, 18, 19, 20, 21, 22, 23, 24, 25, 26, 27, 28, 29, 30, 31, 32, 33, 34, 35, 36, 37, 38, 39, 40, 41, 42, Copper Pyrites ; 43, 44, 45, 46, 47, 48, Black Copper from smelting furnaces ; 49, Smelted Copper from furnace.
   Exhibited by J. Isaac Bennett, Manager, Mount Perry Copper Mines.

4. STREAM TIN AND KAOLIN—
   From the Tinfields of Stanthorpe.
   Exhibited by Queensland Government.

5. BLOCK OF ANTIMONY, SULPHIDE—
   Exhibited by E. Ahrenfeld, Neardie, Wide Bay.

6. CHROME IRON (from near Ipswich)—
   From which the colours were made. (See "Manufactured Products.")
   Exhibited by Queensland Government.

7. PLUMBAGO (from Stanthorpe)—
   Exhibited by Queensland Government.

8. PLUMBAGO (from the Lower Burdekin)—
   Exhibited by R. W. Graham, Lillymere.

9. MINERALS FROM THE RAVENSWOOD GOLDFIELD—
   2 pieces Pyrites, containing 41 oz. 3 dwts. Gold and 9·72 per cent. of Copper ; 1 piece Galena (Silver-bearing, 122 ozs. to the ton).
   Exhibited by Queensland Government.

10. CINNABAR—
    From Kilkivan, near Gympie.
    Exhibited by Captain Eldred.

11. GRANITE (from Northern Queensland)—
    Exhibited by Queensland Government (Honourable J. Doug'as).

12. GRANITE (from Enoggera)—
    Presented by John Petrie.
    Exhibited by Queensland Government.

13. FREESTONE (SANDSTONE)—from Murphy's Creek—
Presented by John Petrie.
Exhibited by Queensland Government.

14. FREESTONE (SANDSTONE)—from Goodna—
Presented by John Petrie.
Exhibited by Queensland Government.

15. FREESTONE (SANDSTONE)—Breakfast Creek—
Presented by John Petrie.
Exhibited by Queensland Government.

16. HARDSTONE (CLAYSTONE PORPHYRY)—from near Brisbane—
Presented by John Petrie.
Exhibited by Queensland Government.

17. MARBLE—
5 pieces from Calliope, 4 pieces from L Island.
Presented by John Petrie.
Exhibited by Queensland Government.

18. 3 BLOCKS MARBLE—
Neighbourhood of Warwick.
Exhibited by Queensland Government.

19. 4 OPALS—
Bulloo River.
Exhibited by Queensland Government.

MANUFACTURED PRODUCTS.

20. INGOTS OF TIN (½ ton)—Smelted at Stanthorpe—
Exhibited by Queensland Government.

21. GRAIN TIN (1 cwt.)—Smelted at Stanthorpe—
Exhibited by Queensland Government.

22. 1 TIN INGOT (84 lbs.)—from the Palmer River—
Exhibited by J. Duncan.

23. REGULUS OF ANTIMONY—
Smelted from Ore of the Wide Bay Mines.
Exhibited by Queensland Government.

24. INGOTS OF COPPER (½ ton)—
From Mount Perry Mines.
Exhibited by Queensland Government.

25. COKE—
From the Coal Mine of Brydon and Co., near Ipswich.
Exhibited by Brydon and Co.

25A. COKE.—James Gulland, Ipswich.

25B. COAL.—James Gulland, Ipswich.

26. COLOURS MADE FROM CHROME IRON—
Found near Ipswich.
Exhibited by Queensland Government.

VARIA.

27. COLLECTION OF FOSSILS—
From Coal Mines near Ipswich. 5 specimens *Pecopteris odontopteroidee*
3 specimens *Filices*, 1 *Cyclopteris*, 36 specimens *P. Australis*
2 *Sphenopteris elongata*, 5 *Sphenopteris* species.
Exhibited by Queensland Government.

VEGETABLE PRODUCTS.

N.B.—Numbers marked in brackets thus ( ) denote the numbers in Special Catalogue
from Botanical Gardens, Brisbane.

I.—Queensland Timbers.

Numbers (1 to 177K) Botanic Garden, Brisbane.

177. Sandalwood (from Cooktown), Honourable J. Douglas, Queensland Government.
178. Kauri Pine (from Noosa), Queensland Government.
178. „ „ „
178. „ „ „
179. Cypress Pine „ „
180. Cedar, 1 specimen Light and 1 Dark (in boards), A. Mackay, Brisbane.

II.—Cereals.

181. Wheat (79), C. Armstrong, Warwick.
182. „ (80) Geo. Bell, Bundaberg.,
183. „ (81), James Hood, Bundaberg.
184. „ (82), C. and S. Hayes, Warwick.
185. „ (83), Walker, R. F., Toowoomba.
186. „ (84), Walker, R. F., Toowoomba.
187. „ (85), Walker, R. F., Toowoomba.
188. „ (86), Price, W., Bundaberg.
189. „ Horwitz and Co., Warwick.
190. Maize (87), Ferguson, W., Coomera.
191. „ (88), Ferguson, W., Coomera.
192. „ (89), Frankland, H., Upper Albert
193. „ (90), Hall, G., Carlton Farm, North Pine.
194. „ (91), Hall, G., Carlton Farm, North Pine.
195. „ (92), Walker, R. F., Toowoomba.
196. „ Horwitz and Co., Warwick.
197. „ Woodward, G., Samson Vale.
198. Malting Barley (93), Walker, R. F., Toowoomba.
199. Oats (94), Walker, R. F., Toowoomba.
200. Rice (95), Botanic Gardens, Brisbane.
201. „ (96), „ „
202. „ (97), „ „
203. „ (98), „ „
204. „ (99), „ „
205. „ (100), „ „

III.—Cotton.

206. Sea Island and Uplands, Mackay, A., Brisbane.

IV.—Tobacco.

207. Leaf (202), Nerang Creek.
208. „ (203), Ipswich Reserve.
209. „ (204), Albert River.
210. „ (205), Pine River.
211. „ (206), Coomera River, Ferguson, W.
212. „ (207), Mahony, J. Cunnungera Creek.
213. „ Hocker and Co., Brisbane.
214. „ Wickham, H. A., Herbert River.

V.—Tea, Coffee, Spices, &c.

215. Tea (101), Botanic Garden, Brisbane—Black Tea.
216.   „ (101A),   „   „   Tea.
217.   „ (103),   „   „   Paraguay Tea.
218.   „ (103A),   „   „   Paraguay Tea or Maté.
219. Coffee Leaves (102), „   „
220.   „   Alexander, W. R., Redbank, prepared as substitute for Tea.
221. Coffee (104), Sandrock, G. R., Bowen.
222.   „   (105), Botanic Garden, Brisbane.
223.   „   (106), Stewart, J., Herbert River.
224.   „   Alexander, W. R., Redbank.
225. Coffee Berry (107), Stewart, J. Gairloch, Herbert River.
226.   „   Alexander, W. R., Redbank.
227. Coffee Bean (108), Williams, A., Logan Road.
228.   „   (109),   „   „
229. Senna (110), Botanic Garden, Brisbane.
230.   „   (111), Botanic Garden, Brisbane.
231. Rosella, dried (112), Botanic Garden, Brisbane.
232. Bananas, dried (113),   „   „
233. Bunya Bunya Nuts (114), Botanic Garden, Brisbane.
234. Queensland Nuts (115), Botanic Garden, Brisbane.
235.   „   (116),   „   „
236. Cycas Media (117), Botanic Gardens, Brisbane.
237. Cinnamon (118), Williams, A., Logan Road.
238. Cayenne Pepper (119), Botanic Garden, Brisbane.
239. Cayenne Pepper (120), Botanic Garden, Brisbane.
240. Cayenne Pepper (121), Botanic Garden, Brisbane.

VI.—Dyeing Materials, Gum Resins and Barks.

241. Madder (123), Botanic Gardens.
242. Logwood (124),   „   „
243. Cockspur (125),   „   „
244. Turmeric (126),   „   „
245. Indigo (127),   „   „
246. Gum Resins.—
246.   Cypress Pine Gum (171), Botanic Garden.
247.   Bloodwood Gum (172),   „   „
248.   Bunya Bunya Gum (173),   „   „
249.   „   Catechu (174), Botanic Garden.
250.   „   Grass-tree Gum (175), Botanic Garden.
251.   „   Bottle-tree Gum (176),   „   „
252. Barks, Blue Gum (177), Botanic Garden.
253.   „   Ironbark (178),   „   „
254.   „   Mangrove (179),   „   „
255.   „   Green Wattle (180), „   „
256.   „   Black Wattle (181), „   „
257.   „   Fever Bark (182),   „   „
258.   „   Crab-tree (183),   „   „

VEGETABLE PRODUCTS (Manufactured).

VII.—Sugars.

259. Sugar, Sheriff of Queensland.
260.   „   Coleridge Mills (1), Dart, W., Brisbane River.
261.   „   „   (2),   „   „

43

262. Sugar, Oxley Creek (3), Donaldson, ——.
263.   „   Richmond (4), Berry, H., Brisbane River.
264.   „   Normanby Mill (4A), Gardner, O.
265.   „   „   (4B),   „
266.   „   „   (4C),   „
267.   „   Ageston Plantation (5), Couldery, W. H., Logan River.
268.   „   „   „   (6),   „   „   „
269.   „   „   „   (7),   „   „   „
270.   „   „   „   (8),   „   „   „
271.   „   „   „   (9),   „   „   „
272.   „   „   „   (10),   „   „   „
273.   „   „   „   (11),   „   „   „
274.   „   Bannockburn (12), Watt, A., Beenleigh.
275.   „   „   (13),   „   „
276.   „   Benowa Plantation (14), Muir, R., Nerang Creek.
277.   „   „   „   (15),   „   „
278.   „   Binibi Plantation (16), Philpott Bros., Nerang Creek.
279.   „   „   „   (17),   „   „
280.   „   Noyea Plantation (18), Gartside, Muir, and Black, Albert.
281.   „   „   „   (19),   „   „   „
282.   „   „   „   (20),   „   „   „
283.   „   Loganholme (21), Fryar, W., Logan River.
284.   „   „   (22),   „   „
285.   „   Otmoor (23), Bank of Queensland, Coomera.
286.   „   „   (24),   „   „
287.   „   Tygum Plantation (25), Lahey and Sons, Logan.
288.   „   Kircubbin (26), Rawson, Lancelot, Maryborough District.
289.   „   Nevada (27), Monckton, H., Maryborough.
290.   „   „   (28),   „   „
291.   „   Yengarie Plantation (29), Tooth and Cran, Maryborough.
292.   „   „   „   (30),   „   „   „
293.   „   „   „   (31),   „   „   „
294.   „   Burnett River (32).
295.   „   Burnett River (33), Shearon.
296.   „   Waterview (34), Johnston, S., Bundaberg.
297.   „   Mackay (35), Watts, Mackay District.
298.   „   Alexandra Plantation (36), Davidson, J. E.
299.   „   Balmoral Plantation (37), Hyne and Co.
300.   „   Barrie Plantation (38),
301.   „   Branscombe Plantation (39), King, H. M.
302.   „   Cassada Plantation (40), Mackay District.
303.   „   Cedars Plantation (41),   „
304.   „   Dumbleton Plantation (42),   „
305.   „   Foulden Plantation (43),   „
306.   „   Meadowlands Plantation (44),   „
307.   „   „   „   (44A),   „
308.   „   Miclere Plantation (45),   „
309.   „   Nebia Plantation (46),   „
310.   „   Inverness Plantation (47),   „
311.   „   Pleystowe Plantation (48),   „
312.   „   Pioneer Plantation (49),   „
313.   „   River Estate (50),   „
314.   „   Te Kowai Plantation (51)   „
315.   „   „   „   (52),   „
316.   „   „   „   (53),   „
317.   „   Meadowlands Estate (54),   „
318.   „   „   „   (55),   „
319.   „   „   „   (56),   „

320. Sugar, Mackinade Plantation (57), Neame and Co., Herbert River
321.   „   „   „   (58),   „   „
322.   „   „   „   (59),   „   „
323.   „   Mackinade Plantation—Neame and Co., Herbert River.
323.   „   „   „   „   „
324.   „   Watt, A., Beenleigh.
325.   „   Dart, Wm., Indooroopilly.
326.   „   Dart, Wm.,   „
327.   „   Bundall Plantation—Holland Miskin and Co., Nerang Creek.
328.   „   „   „   „   „
339.   „   „   „   „   „
330.   „   „   „   „   „
331.   „   Pioneer Plantation—Spiller, J., Mackay.
332.   „   Ashburton Estate—   „   „
333.   „   River Estate—   „   „
334.   „   Richmond Estate—   „   „
335.   „   Alexandra,   §1—Mackenzie, James (Chairman Mackay District Association).

336.   „   „   §2—   „
337.   „   Branscombe,   §1—   „
338.   „   „   §2—   „
339.   „   Nebia,   §1—   „
340.   „   „   §2—   „
341.   „   Dumbleton,   §1—   „
342.   „   „   §2—   „
343.   „   Cedars,   §1—   „
344.   „   „   §2—   „
345.   „   Meadowlands, §1—   „
346.   „   „   §2—   „
347.   „   Barrie   —   „
348.   „   Te Kowai   —   „
349.   „   Lionel Duval, Nebia, §1 & 2 „

VIII.—Farinas.

350. Wheaten Flour, (61) Hayes and Co., Warwick.
351.   „   (62) Kates and Co., Allora.
352.   „   Horwitz and Co , Warwick.
353. Rye Flour,   (62A) Kates and Co., Allora.
354. Wheaten Meal (63) Hayes and Co., Warwick.
355.   „   (64) Honourable W. Pettigrew, Brisbane.
356. Maizemeal (65), Honourable W. Pettigrew,
357.   „   Horwitz and Co., Warwick.
358. Arrowroot (66), Shaorrcks, T., Bundaberg.
359.   „   (67), Botanic Garden, Brisbane.
360.   „   (68),   „   „
361.   „   (69), Hall, J., Carlton Farm, North Pine River.
362.   „   (70), Lahey and Son, Tygum, Logan River.
363.   „   (71), Mills, J., Pimpama.
364.   „   Lahey and Sons, Pimpama.
365.   „   Lane, H., North Pine.
366. Ground Rice (72), Botanic Garden, Brisbane.
367. Cassava, sweet (73),   „   „
368.   „   bitter (74),   „   „
369. Zamia Flour (75),   „   „
370. Arrowroot   (76), Burnett, J., Burpengary.
371.   „   (77),   „   „
372. Tapioca   (78),   „

IX.—Fibres.

373. Jute (128), Botanic Garden, Brisbane—Corchorus capsularis (*Linn.*).
374. „ (128A), „ „ — „
375. „ (129), „ „ —Corchorus olitorius (*Linn.*)
376. „ (129A), „ „ — „
377. Rosella Hemp (130), Botanic Garden, Brisbane—Hibiscus sabdariffa (*Linn.*).
378. „ „ (131), „ „ „
379. Sunn Hemp (132), Botanic Garden—Crotalaria juncea (*Linn.*)
380. Pita Hemp (133), „ —Agave americana (*Linn.*)
381. Mexican Hemp (134), „ —Fourcroya gigantea (*Vent.*)
382. Hibiscus Mutabilis (135), „ —Hibiscus mutabilis (*Linn.*)
383. White Mulberry (136), „ —Morus alba (*Linn.*)
384. Queensland Hemp (137), „ —Sida retusa (*Linn.*)
385. „ (138A), „ „
386. „ (139), „ „
387. Vacoa or Screw Pine (140), „ —Pandanus utilis (*Bojer.*)
388. Agave, Sp. (141), „ — „
389. Adam's Needle Fibre (142), „ —Yucca gloriosa (*Willd.*)
390. Silk Grass Fibre (143), „ —Yucca alœfolia (*Linn.*)
391. Dracæna-disco Linn (144), „
392. Cuba Bast (145), „ —Paritium elatum (*Don.*)
393. Bowstrung Hemp (146), „ —Sanseviera Zeylanica, (*Willd.*)
394. Vacoa or Screw Pine (147), „ —Pandanus utilis (*Bojer.*)
395. Flax, Q. (148), „ —Linum usitatissimum Linn.
396. New Zealand Flax (149), „ —Phormium tenax (*Forst.*)
397. Cordage made from Linum „ usitatissimum Linn (150),
398. Cordage made from Queens- „ —Sida retusa. land Hemp (150A)
399. Short Staple Cotton (150B) „ —Gossypium herbaceum (*Linn.*)
400. Brisbane Short Staple Cotton, (150c), Botanic Garden—Gossypium herbaceum (*Linn.*)
401. Abutilon oxycarpum (medium shrub), Malvaceæ, Eaves, S. H. Brisbane.
402. Calanthe veratrifolia (herbaceous plant), Orchideæ „ „
403. Colocasia macrorrhiza (herbaceous plant), Aroideæ „ „
404. Commersonia echinata (small tree), Sterculiaceæ „ „
405. Commersonia Fraseri (medium tree), Sterculiaceæ „ „
406. Corchorus Cunninghamii (herbaceous plant), Tiliaceæ „ „
407. Cordyline cannæfolia (small palm-like tree), Liliaceæ „ „
408. Corypha australis (large palm-tree), Palmæ „ „
409. Crotalaria Mitchelli (herbaceous plant), Leguminosæ „ „
410. Cymbidium suave (herbaceous plant), Orchideæ „ „
411. Cyperus vaginatus (herbaceous plant), Cyperaceæ „ „
412. Dendrobium Hillii (herbaceous plant), Orchideæ „ „
413. Dianella cœrulea (herbaceous plant), Liliaceæ „ „
414. Doryanthes Palmeri (large herbaceous plant), „ „ Amarillideæ
415. Dracæna australis (small palm-like tree), Liliaceæ „ „
416. Dracæna nutans „ „ „ „ „
417. Eucalyptus amygdalina (large tree), Myrtaceæ „ „
418. „ corymbosa „ „ „ „
419. „ obliqua „ „ „ „
420. „ obtusiflora „ „ „ „
421. „ pilularis „ „ „ „

422.	Eucalyptus robusta (large tree), Mytercex, Eaves, S. H., Brisbane.
423.	Ficus aspera (medium tree), Urticeæ		,,	,,
424.	„ australis (large tree) „		,,	,,
425.	„ macrophylla „ „		,,	,,
426.	„ syringæfolia „ „		,,	,,
427.	Flagellaria australis (large climber), Liliaceæ, Eaves, S. H., Brisbane.
428.	Flagellaria indica (large climber), Liliaceæ,		,,	,,
429.	Hibiscus, Fraserii (small tree), Malvaceæ,		,,	,,
430.	„ heterophyllus (small tree) Malvaceæ,		,,	,,
431.	„ Richardsonii (large shrub), „		,,	,,
432.	„ splendens (small tree), Malvaceæ,		,,	,,
433.	„ tiliaceus (medium tree),		,,	,,
434.	Lagunaria Patersonii (medium tree), Malvaceæ,		,,	,,
435.	Laportea moroides (large tree), Urticeæ,		,,	,,
436.	„ gigas (large tree), Urticeæ,		,,	,,
437.	„ photiniphylla (large tree), Urticeæ,		,,	,,
438.	Melaleuca ericifolia (medium tree), Myrtaceæ,		,,	,,
439.	„ styphelioides (large tree), „		,,	,,
440.	Pandanus spiralis (medium palm-like tree),		,,	,,
	Pandaneæ
441.	Pipturus argenteus (medium tree), Urticeæ,		,,	,,
442.	Plagianthus pulchellus (medium tree), Malvaceæ		,,	,,
443.	Seaforthia elegans (large palm), Palmæ		,,	,,
444.	Sesbania aculeata (herbaceous plant), Leguminosæ,		,,	,,
445.	Sida rhombifolia (small shrub), Malvaceæ,		,,	,,
446.	Sterculia acerifolia (large tree), Sterculiaceæ,		,,	,,
447.	„ discolor (large tree),		,,	,,
448.	„ diversifolia (medium tree), Sterculiaceæ,		,,	,,
449.	„ quadrifida (medium tree), „		,,	,,
450.	Trema aspera (large shrub), Urticeæ,		,,	,,
451.	Xerotes longifolia (herbaceous plant), Xerotideæ,		,,	,,
452.	„ Brownii (herbaceous plant), „ „		,,
453.	Ficus macrophylla, Macpherson, Alex., Brisbane.
454.	Ficus rubiginosa,		,,	,,
455.	Corchorus capsularis,		,,	,,
456.	Sida retusa (S. rhombifolia),		,,	,,
457.	Hibiscus tiliaceus,		,,	,,
458.	Hibiscus sorbifolia,		,,	,,
459.	Hibiscus mutabilis,		,,	,,
460.	Hibiscus heterophyllus,		,,	,,
461.	Hibiscus splendens,		,,	,,
462.	Phormium tenax,		,,	,,
463.	Xerotes longifolia,		,,	.,
464.	Agave Americana,		,,	,,
465.	Agave Americana variegata,		,,	,,
466.	Fourcroya gigantea,		,,	,,
467.	Abutilan oxycarpum,		,,	,,
468.	Dracæna draco,		,,	,,
469.	Dracæna australis,		,,	,,
470.	Pandanus utilis,		,,	,,
471.	Pandanus spiralis,		,,	,,
472.	Yucca alœifolia,		,,	,,
473.	Yucca gloriosa,		,,	,,
474.	Keraudrenia Hookeriana,		,,	,,
475.	Agave dwarf,		,,	,,
476.	Ananassa sativa,		,,	,,
477.	Ananassa sativa, B.,		,,	,,
478	Musa maculata,		,,	,

479.	Musa superba,	MacPherson, Alexander, Brisbane.
480.	Musa purpurea,	,, ,,
481.	Seaforthia elegans (palm)	,, ,,
482.	Raphia Ruffia	,, ,,
483.	Commersonia echinata	,, ,,
484.	Bambusa arundinacea	,, ,,
485.	Canna edulis	,, ,,
486.	Gahnia aspera	,, ,,
487.	Xerotes Brownii	,, ,,
488.	Cordyline cannæfolia	,, ,,
489.	Dianella cærulea	,, ,,
490.	Cymbidium suave	,, ,,
491.	Flagellaria indica	,, ,,
492.	Juncus communis	,, ,,
493.	Abroma augusta	,, ,,
494.	Dombeya masterii	,, ,,
495.	Linum usitatissimum	,, :,
496.	Linum (C)	,, ,,
497.	Laportea gigas	,, ,,
498.	Abutilon, sp.	,, ,,
499.	Sanseviera cylindrica	,, ,,

X.—Manufactured Tobacco.

500. Tobacco (198), Soegaard, H., Nindooinbah
501.   ,,   (200)   ,,   ,,
502.   ,,   Hocker and Co., Brisbane
503. Cigars (199), Soegaard, H., Nindooinbah
504.   ,,   (201)   ,,   ,,
505.   ,,   Hocker and Co., Brisbane
506. Cigarettes, Hocker and Co., Brisbane

XI.—Essential Oils, Tinctures, &c.

507.	Oil of Blue Gum	(151),	Botanic Garden
508.	Tincture of Crabtree	(152)	,,
509.	Essence of Verbena	(153)	,,
510.	Tincture of Red Gum	(154)	,,
511.	Essence of Jasmine	(155)	,,
512.	Essence of Acacia	(156)	,,
513.	Oil of Orange	(157)	,,
514.	Tincture of Gelsemium	(158)	,,
515.	Tincture of Bitter Bark	(159)	,,
516.	Orange Bitters	(160)	,,
517.	Hyapana Bitters	(161)	,,
518.	Liquid annatto	(162)	,,
519.	Quassia	(164)	,,
520.	Tamarinds	(165)	,,
521.	Castor Oil	(167)	,,
522.	Ipecacuanha	(168)	,,

523. Croton Oil (169), Botanic Garden.
524. Oil of Lemon (170), Botanic Garden.
525. Pitcheri (170A), Botanic Garden.
526. Oil, extracted from Ironbark (Eucalyptus).   Queensland Government.
     (Prepared by K. T. Staiger, F.L.S.)

XI a.

527. Wines, Lade, J. J., Samford Road—3 bottles Dry Red, 3 bottles Sweet
     Red, 3 bottles Sweet White, 3 bottles Dry White.

528. Wines, Irwin, Brothers, Warrilla—A 3 bottles White, 1874-5; B 3 bottles Warrilla White, 1875-6; C and D 6 bottles Warrilla Red, 1874-6.
529. „ Beavan, W., Gatton—3 bottles Rosella Wine, 4 years old.
5 30. „ Lambert, G., Indooroopilly—1 bottle White, and 3 bottles Red Wines.
531. Spirits—Rum (183), Couldery, W. H., Ageston.
532. „ „ (185), Gardner, O., Normanby Distillery.
533. „ „ (186), „ „ „
534. „ „ (187), „ „ „
535. „ „ (188), „ „ „
536. „ „ (189), „ ·, „
537. „ ·, (190), „ „ „

538.—XII.—Indigenous Pasture·Grasses and Fodder Plants.

Andropogon annulatus, Forsk.	(208)	Botanic Gardens.
„ acicularis, Betz.	(209)	„
„ erianthoides, F. M.	(210)	„
„ Gryllus, Linn.	(211)	„
„ halepensis, Sib.	(212)	„
„ montanus, Roxb.	(213)	„
„ nervosus, Rott.	(214)	„
„ pertusus, Willd.	(215)	„
„ refractus, R. B.	(216)	„
„ rottbœlloides, Steud.	(217)	„
„ triticeus, R. B.	(218)	„
Agrostis Solandri, F. M.	(219)	„
Anthistiria australis, R. B.	(220)	„
„ arenacea, F. M.	(221)	„
„ ciliata, L.	(222)	„
„ membranacea, Lindl.	(223)	„
Arundinella nepalensis, Trin.	(224)	„
Chloris divaricata, R. B.	(225)	„
„ ventricosa, R. B.	(226)	„
„ scariosa, F. M.	(227)	„
Cynodon Dactylon, Pers.	(228)	„
Danthonia pectinata, Lindl.	(229)	„
„ lappacea, Lindl.	(230)	„
Eleusine indica, Gœrt.	(231)	„
Festuca Billardierii, Steud.	(232)	„
Helopus annulatus, Nees.	(233)	„
Imperata arundinacea, Cyr.	(234)	„
Microlœna stipoides, R. B.	(235)	„
Panicum coloratum, Linn.	(236)	„
Panicum lœvinode, Lindl.	(237)	„
Panicum parviflorum, R. B.	(238)	„
Panicum crusgalli, Linn.	(239)	„
Panicum decompositum, R. B.	(240)	„
Panicum hispidulum, Retz.	(241)	„
Panicum virgatum, Linn.	(242)	„
Panicum italicum, L.	(243)	„
Poa Brownii, Nees.	(244)	„
Poa cæspitosa, Nees.	(245)	„
Poa parviflora, R. B.	(246)	„
Poa chinensis, Kœnig.	(247)	„
Perotis rara, R. B.	(248)	„
Sporobolus indicus, R. B.	(249)	„

Sporobolus elongatus, R. B. (250) Botanic Gardens.
Stipa Dichelachne, Steud. (251) „
Stipa ramosissima, Sieb. (252) „
Daucus brachiatus, Sieb. (353) „
Apium leptophyllum, F. M. (254) „
Plantago varia, R. B. (255) „
Chenopodium auricomum, Lindl. (256) „
Rhagodia parabolica, Br. (257) „
Atriplex semibaccata, R. B. (258) „
Atriplex vesicaria, Hew. (259) „
Atriplex, Spe. (260) „

XIII.—Herbarium.

,539. 4 Volumes illustrative of the Botany of Queensland—Queensland Government (F. M. Bailey).

XIV.—Miscellaneous.

540. Midgeen Canes (191) Botanic Garden.
541. „ (191A) „
542. Cardwell Cane (192) „
543. Mackay Bean (194) ,'
544. Bottle of Limejuice (195) Hall, S., Carlton Farm.
545. Egg-stand and Cups (196)
546. Bitter Cups (197)
547. Maps of parts of Queensland—Queensland Government (W. Knight).
548. Photographic Views of Queensland—Queensland Government.

ANIMAL PRODUCTS.

1. Wool, Gore and Co., Yandilla, Darling Downs.—Washed Wool, hoggetts, 12 months' growth; spout-washed in cold water.
2. „ Gunn, D., Pikedale.—
    Washed—No. 1 Clothing, No. 2 Combing, No. 3 Clothing, Hoggetts, No. 4 Combing, Hoggetts.
    Greasy—No. 5 Combing, Hoggetts, No. 6 Clothing, Hoggetts, No. 7 Clothing, No. 8 Combing.
3. „ Hodgson and Ramsay, Eton Vale.—Greasy—Clothing, Ewes.
4. „ Clark, G., Hendon, East Talgai.—Greasy—Australian Merinos.
5. „ Marshall and Slade, Glengallan, No. 3.—
    No. 1. 4 Rams' fleeces, 2 and 3 years, pure Merinos; Combing.
    No. 2. 6 Breeding Ewes' fleeces, Greasy, pure Merinos, 3 to 6 years; Combing.
6. „ Tooth, W. B., Clifton.—(3 cases.)
7. „ Marked EFG, 1 case, 6 fleeces.
8. Mohair, Clark, C., Hendon, East Talgai.
9. Specimens of Silk (122), Botanic Gardens, Brisbane.
10. „ „ Sheriff of Queensland.
11. Silk Cocoons, Sheriff of Queensland.
12. Kangaroo and other skins, Stephens, A., South Brisbane.—2 dozen Kangaroo and 12$\frac{A}{12}$ dozen Wallaby, Wallaroo, and Paddy Melon skins.
13. „ „ McGlynn, Kelvin Grove.—2 dozen Kangaroo and 2 dozen Wallaby skins.
14 „ „ Queensland Government, Darling Downs.—8 dozen Kangaroo and mixed skins (green).

15. Bêche de Mer, Beardmore and Olive, Cooktown.
16. Pearl Shell, Queensland Government, from Townsville. Pearl Shell, by Honourable J. Douglas, Torres Straits.
17. Dugong Oil (122), Botanic Gardens, Brisbane.
18.   „   Berkley, Taylor, and Co., Brisbane.
19.   „   Stiller, F. K., Moreton Bay.
20.   „   Ching, J. L., Hervey's Bay, Maryborough.—A. 12 bottles with stearine. B. 12 bottles without stearine.
21. Dugong Hide, Ching, J. L., Hervey's Bay Fisheries, Maryborough.— ½ side of Dugong hide.

ANIMAL PRODUCTS (Manufactured).

22. Saddles—Hill, J., Kedron Brook.
23. Soap—Ruddell, R., Bundaberg—Household Soap, value £30 per ton.
24. Preserved Meat—Whitehead and Co.—Fitzroy Meat Preserving Establishment, Rockhampton.

Miscellaneous.

25. Bones of Dugong—Ching, J. L., Hervey's Bay Fisheries, Maryborough —A1, Skull of Adult Dugong Bull ; B2, Skull of Adult Dugong Cow ; c3, Skull of Dugong Calf ; D4, Rib-bones of Adult Dugong ; E5, Tusks of Adult Dugong ; F6, Set of Views of one of Fishery Camps.
26. Collection of Native Weapons—Honourable A. H. Palmer, Fernberg, Brisbane.
27. Collection of Native Weapons, A. J. Boyd, Milton.
28. Collection of Native Weapons—Ruddle, W., Fortitude Valley, Brisbane.
29. Filter—Shepherd, T., Bundanba, near Ipswich.

APPENDICES.

CATALOGUE OF THE TIMBERS OF QUEENSLAND, COLLECTED AND ARRANGED BY WALTER HILL, BOTANIC GARDEN, BRISBANE.

The Timbers of Queensland.

OWING in some measure to the vast area of Queensland, but principally to the diversity of its soil, climate, and altitude, there are perhaps a greater variety of indigenous timber-yielding trees than are to be met with in any of the other Australian Colonies. The deep ravines and sheltered valleys, and the high mountain sides even in the same latitude, furnish different varieties of timber; and again, the same varieties grown in different situations and under different climatic influences, present a different appearance.

The specimens exhibited are chosen chiefly for their economic value. The list, however, does not include one-fourth of the species that have already been described, and there are also many that have not yet been classified. Each district of this immense territory is characterised by features in its vegetation peculiar to itself, and years must elapse before they are all known and botanically arranged.

On the north-east coast a rich field for scientific investigation exists, even if it were confined to timbers of strictly economic value. Very many trees that are known in other parts of Australia are to be found there, together with those that are peculiar to Queensland, and our knowledge of the latter would, no doubt, be largely increased were the country explored with a view to ascertaining its natural vegetable wealth. This would doubtless be the case were a stimulus afforded by the opening-up of an export trade. Before this can be accomplished, it is requisite that samples of the timbers, a description of their uses and qualities, together with the market price (where possible), should be accessible to purchasers. With this object in view the present collection has been formed.

It appears inseparable, from the state of affairs in a young colony, that very little time or trouble should be devoted to experiment, or to the improvement of existing processes. The same timbers that the first settlers made use of, are still employed as a matter of course for the same purposes, and timbers in many instances of a superior description, are neglected or used only as firewood.

It will be for the practical builder, the shipwright, and the cabinet-maker, to pronounce an opinion upon the qualities of the timbers represented, and it is probable that many of them will have a greater value placed upon them than they receive in Queensland.

The value of some descriptions of the Australian Eucalypti for building and railway purposes has been for some time past fully recognised, and the number of species in Queensland is greater than in other parts of Australia. But, at the same time, there appears to be but little doubt that many of the Eucalypti produce timber so much alike, that one piece cannot well be distinguished from another, even when obtained from trees having well defined botanical distinctions. In addition to this genera, there are a variety of timbers that are remarkable for their strength, durability, fineness of grain, or ornamental appearance, which renders many of them eminently adapted for the purposes of the cabinet maker.

Wherever it is possible, the price for which these timbers can be delivered alongside, ready for shipment, is given, and where such is not the case, a slight advance on the price of Eucalyptus timber may be quoted, unless the timber is small and not of frequent occurrence, and if persons in the trade are desirous of making definite offers for a supply of these timbers, they are—requested to communicate with the Agent-General, who will afford them the requisite information.

———

CATALOGUE OF THE TIMBERS OF QUEENSLAND.

CONIFERÆ.

1. *Araucaria Bidwilli*, Hook. (Bunya Bunya).—Diameter, 30 to 48 inches; height, 100 to 200 feet. A noble tree, inhabiting the scrubs in the district between the Brisbane and the Burnett Rivers. In the twenty-seventh parallel it grows thickly over a portion of country, in extent about thirty miles long by twelve broad. The timber is not only very strong and good, but it is full of beautiful veins, and capable of being polished and worked with the greatest facility. The cones produced on the upper branches, with the apex downwards, are large, measuring 9 to 12 inches in length and 10 inches in diameter.

2. *Araucaria Cunninghamii*, Ait. (Moreton Bay Pine).—Diameter, 36 to 66 inches; height, 150 to 200 feet. This is one of the most useful trees in Queensland. It covers immense tracts of land along the coast and in the interior. The timber is an article of great commercial importance, and is extensively used in the colony, and a considerable quantity exported to the southern colonies. The timber is strong and durable when kept dry, and is also very durable in the bottoms of vessels when kept constantly wet, but soon decays when exposed to alternate damp and dryness. When procured from the mountains in the interior it is fine-grained and is susceptible of a high polish, which excels that of satinwood or bird's-eye maple. The market value a the present time is from 55s. to 70s. per thousand superficial feet.

3. *Dammara robusta*, Moore (Kaurie or Dundathu Pine).—Diameter, 36 to 72 inches; height, 80 to 130 feet. This fine tree inhabits the alluvial banks on rivers near the coast, in the Wide Bay District principally. The timber is fine-grained, free from knots, and easily worked. The market value at the present time is 70s. per thousand superficial feet.

4. *Callitris columellaris*, F. M. (Cypress Pine).—Diameter, 20 to 40 inches; height, 50 to 70 feet. This tree forms vast tracts along the coast, growing on barren sandy soils. The timber is an article of great importance; it is durable, fine-grained, fragrant, and capable of a high polish; it is used for piles of wharves and for sheathing punts and boats; it resists the attacks of cobra and white ants, and the root is valued by cabinet-makers for veneering purposes. The market value at the present time is 120s. per thousand superficial feet.

5. *Callitris verrucosa*, R. B. (the Desert Cypress Pine).—Diameter, 12 to 24 inches; height, 50 to 70 feet. A handsome tree, scattered through the sandy ridges of the Darling Downs District. The timber is much used by the settlers for building purposes.

5A. See No. 173.

6. *Podocarpus elata*, R. B. (She-pine).—Diameter, 20 to 36 inches; height, 50 to 80 feet. A very beautiful tree, trunk rarely cylindrical, timber free from knots, soft, close, easily worked; good for joiner's work, and used for spars. It occurs very frequently in the scrubs along the coast. The market value at the present time is about 65s. to 70s. per thousand feet superficial.

6A. See No. 174.

CASUARINEÆ.

7. *Casuarina tenuissima*, Sieb. (River Oak).—Diameter, 18 to 22 inches; height, 40 to 70 feet. Found growing only in or near the borders of creeks; the timber is strong and tough, used for staves and shingles.

8. *Casuarina leptoclada*, Miq. (Erect She-oak).—Diameter, 9 to 18 inches; height, 20 to 35 feet. Small tree, timber close, prettily marked, but not very durable.

9. *Casuarina equisetifolia*, Forst. (Swamp Oak).—Diameter, 12 to 24 inches; height, 50 to 70 feet. Found growing in great abundance near salt-water marshes and inlets. The wood is close-grained and beautifully marked, and is used for purposes where lightness and toughness are required.

10. *Casuarina torulosa*, Ait. (Forest Oak).—Diameter, 9 to 18 inches; height, 30 to 40 feet. A small tree occupying large tracts of land in the open forest. The timber is much used for fuel, it is close and prettily marked, and gives handsome veneers.

10A. See No. 175.

MELIACEÆ.

11. *Cedrela Toona*, Roxb. (Red Cedar).—Diameter 24 to 76 inches; height, 100 to 150 feet. This magnificent deciduous tree is found in scrubs along the coast, and occasionally extending inland for a considerable distance. It puts out large branches, the junctions of which with the stem, furnish those beautiful curled pieces of which the choicest veneers are made. The timber is light, very durable, and easily worked, and is largely employed in house-joinery, and furniture-making, in fact, whenever lightness and durability are required. It is an article of great commercial importance, and is largely exported to the other colonies. The market value at the present time is from 150s. to 170s. per thousand superficial feet, according to colour and size.

12. *Flindersia australis*, R. B. (Flindosa).—Diameter, 36 to 48 inches; height, 80 to 100 feet. A robust tree of general occurrence in the scrubs on the banks of rivers. The timber is hard, close, and of great strength, and durability, and would make excellent timber for railway purposes. It shrinks very little in drying, and does not rust iron. It has long been known to timber merchants as being a very hard timber, and difficult to cut with the saw, and for that reason little attention has been paid to procuring it.

13. *Flindersia Oxleyana* F. M. (Light Yellowwood).—Diameter, 24 to 42 inches; height, 80 to 100 feet. This fine tree is found in the same situations as red cedar. The timber is strong, durable, fine-grained, and of good colour, used in boat-building, cabinet-work, and for many of the purposes to which cedar is applied. It also possesses dyeing properties. The present market value is from 80s. to 90s. per thousand superficial feet.

14. *Flindersia Bennettiana* F. M. (Bogum Bogum).—Diameter, 18 to 26 inches; height, 70 to 90 feet. A large smooth-stemmed tree. Timber close-grained and durable.

15. *Flindersia maculosa* F. M. (Spotted tree).—Diameter, 12 to 20 inches; height, 30 to 40 feet. Middle-sized tree, timber close-grained and durable, plentiful in the Rosewood scrubs of the Darling Downs district.

16. *Owenia venosa* F. M. (Sour Plum).—Diameter, 9 to 18 inches; height, 30 to 40 feet. A moderate-sized tree common in the Brigalow scrubs in the Darling Downs district. Its great strength renders it suitable for many purposes.

17. *Owenia cerasifera* F. M. (Sweet Plum).—Diameter, 9 to 18 inches; height, 25 to 35 feet. A small but very beautiful tree, timber hard, and of a dark-red colour, finely marked, and takes a very high polish.

18. *Amoora nitidula* (Benth).—Diameter, 18 to 30 inches; height, 70 to 90 feet. A large-sized tree of frequent occurrence in scrubs bordering the coast. Qualities of the timber not much known.

19. *Synoum glandulosum* (A. Juss).—Diameter, 15 to 24 inches; height, 35 to 60 feet, A moderate-sized tree of very general occurrence. Timber firm, and easily worked.

20. *Dysoxylon Muelleri*, Benth. (Pencil Cedar).—Diameter, 20 to 40 inches; height, 70 to 90 feet. A large-sized tree inhabiting the rich alluvial scrubs upon the banks of the rivers in the districts of Moreton Bay and Wide Bay. Timber of a red colour, used for cabinet-making and in-door work. When fresh cut the timber has much the smell of a Swedish turnip. Market value from 100s. to 120s. per thousand superficial feet.

21. *Melia composita*, Willd. (White Cedar).—Diameter, 20 to 36 inches; height, 70 to 80 feet. A middle-sized deciduous tree, in some instances a large tree, never ranging very far from the coast. Timber soft, and easily worked; not in very good repute, though undeservedly, as the timber from a well-matured tree is found to be very durable.

RUTACEÆ.

22. *Bosistoa sapindiformis*, F. M.—Diameter, 6 to 12 inches; height, 15 to 20 feet. Small but very handsome tree; wood close, and light.

23. *Citrus australis*, Planch. (Native Orange).—This tree grows in abundance in the borders of scrubs, both on the coast and in the interior. The timber is hard, close-grained, and of a light-yellow colour.

24. *Citrus australasica*, F. M. (Native Lime).—Diameter, 6 to 10 inches; height, 15 to 20 feet. A low-sized tree found in the scrubs on the Brisbane and Pine Rivers. The timber is close-grained, hard, and of a yellow colour.

25. *Atalantia glauca*, Hook. (Native Cumquat).—Diameter, 2 to 8 inches; height, 8 to 15 feet. Found in great abundance in the Darling Downs and Maranoa Districts. The wood is close-grained and takes a fine polish.

26. *Acronychia Baueri*, Schott.—Diameter, 6 to 12 inches; height, 16 to 24 feet. Small-sized tree, found in great abundance in most of the scrubs bordering the coast; wood close-grained, but not used.

27. *Acronychia imperforata*, F. M.—Diameter, 16 to 20 inches; height, 20 to 40 feet. A middle-sized tree, occurring in the scrubs bordering the Brisbane River. Timber fine-grained, easily worked, but not much used.

28. *Acronychia lævis*, Forst.—Diameter, 15 to 20 inches; height, 30 to 50 feet. A tall, slender tree; timber not used.

29. *Pentaceras australis*, Hook. (White Cedar).—Diameter, 12 to 24 inches; height, 40 to 70 feet. Occurs principally in the scrubs near the coast. The timber is close-grained, tough, and firm.

30. *Zanthoxylum brachyacanthum*, F. M. (Satinwood).—Diameter, 6 to 9 inches; height, 20 to 30 feet. Found in small quantities in most of the scrubs of Queensland. The timber is close-grained, of a yellow colour, and susceptible of a high polish.

31. *Geijera parviflora*, Lindl.—Diameter, 6 to 12 inches; height, 20 to 30 feet. Tree occurring in many of the brigalow scrubs. Timber hard and close-grained; it is, however, apt to split in seasoning.

32. *Geijera Muelleri*, Benth.—Diameter, 12 to 18 inches; height, 40 to 60 feet. Dispersed through the Araucaria scrubs, near Ipswich. The timber is nicely marked, and of agreeable fragrance when green.

CELASTRINEÆ.

33. *Celastrus dispermus*, F. M.—Diameter, 3 to 6 inches; height, 12 to 18 feet. Timber close grained, and takes a fine polish.
34. *Siphonodon australe*, Benth.—Diameter, 12 to 24; height, 40 to 60 feet. Handsome tree of frequent occurrence; wood close grained, of a yellowish colour.
35. *Denhamia pittosporoides*, F. M.—Diameter 6 to 8 inches; height, 20 to 30 feet. Slender tree, found on the borders of scrubs, inland; timber is hard, fine-grained, and takes a good polish.
36. *Denhamia obscura*, Meisn.—Diameter, 3 to 6 inches; height, 12 to 20 feet. Small tree found in the brigalow scrubs, near Ipswich. Wood fine-grained, and tough.
37. *Elæodendron australe*, Vent.—Diameter, 4 to 12 inches; height, 20 to 30 feet. Slender-growing tree. Timber close-grained, and prettily marked.

RHAMNEÆ.

38. *Alphitonia excelsa*, Reissek. (Mountain Ash).—Diameter, 18 to 24 inches; height, 45 to 80 feet. This valuable tree is plentiful in the forest and in the scrubs, both on the coast and in the interior. The timber is hard, close-grained, and durable; takes a high polish, and is suitable for gun-stocks and a variety of other purposes.

PITTOSPOREÆ.

39. *Pittosporum rhombifolium*, A. Cunn.—Diameter, 6 to 12 inches; height, 45 to 55 feet. Found in scrubs on the Brisbane River. The wood is of a white colour, not used.
40. *Pittosporum bicolor*, Hook.—Diameter, 6 to 12 inches; height, 20 to 40 feet. Found in open forest ground in West Moreton and Darling Downs. Wood close-grained, of a white colour.
41. *Pittosporum phillyræoides*, D. C.—Diameter, 4 to 6 inches; height, 20 to 35 feet. Met with in brigalow scrubs; wood close-grained, and of a white colour.

CAPPARIDEÆ.

42. *Capparis nobilis*, F. M. (Native Pomegranate).—Diameter, 6 to 14 inches; height, 20 to 35 feet. A small tree. The timber is hard and close-grained.
43. *Capparis Mitchelli*.—Lindl. wild native pomegranate; diameter, 10 to 12 inches; height, 14 to 30 feet. Found in the brigalow scrubs in the Darling Downs district. The timber is hard and close-grained.
44. *Apophyllum anomalum*, F. M.—Diameter, 6 to 10 inches; height, 20 to 30 feet. Found in the brigalow scrubs in the Darling Downs district. Wood very hard.
44A. See No. 170.

STERCULIACEÆ.

45. *Sterculia quadrifida*, R. B.—Diameter, 18 to 24 inches; height, 40 to 60 feet. Moderate-sized tree; wood soft and spongy; bark used for nets and fishing lines.
46. *Tarrietia argyrodendron*, Benth.—Silver hue; diameter, 24 to 34 inches; height, 70 to 90 feet. A large tree, growing in great quantities in the scrubs bordering the banks of the river. The timber is not much used.

47. *Tarrietia actinodendron,* F. M.—Diameter, 18 to 30 inches ; height, 60 to 70 feet. Plentiful in the coast scrubs ; timber is tough and close-grained, but seldom used.

LINEÆ.

48. *Erythroxylon australe,* F. M.—Diameter, 6 to 12 inches ; height, 20 to 30 feet. Small-sized trees are found in considerable abundance in the brigalow scrub near Ipswich. Timber hard, fine-grained, takes a good polish, and can be used for cabinet-work.

SAPINDACEÆ.

49. *Cupania xylocarpa,* A. Cunn.—Diameter, 12 to 24 inches ; height, 40 to 60 feet. Moderate-sized tree, in good situations. Timber close-grained and hard, particularly so when dry.
50. *Cupania serrata,* F. M.—Diameter, 8 to 14 inches ; height, 20 to 30 feet. Plentiful in the scrubs on the banks of rivers. Timber close-grained.
51. *Diploglottis Cunninghamii,* Hook. (native tamarind.)—Diameter 12 to 24 inches ; height, 40 to 55 feet. Timber seldom used, though compact and durable.
52. *Cupania semiglauca,* F. M.—Diameter, 10 to 20 inches ; height, 30 to 60 feet. Middle-sized tree. Wood soft, and as yet of no recognised value.
53. *Cupania anacardioides,* A. Rich.—Diameter 12 to 18 inches ; height, 30 to 40 feet. Slender tree, in considerable abundance on the alluvial banks of rivers. Timber seldom used.
54. *Cupania pseudorhus,* A. Rich.—Diameter, 14 to 20 inches ; height, 30 to 50 feet. Tree of moderate size, growing in great abundance in the scrubs bordering the coast ; timber fine-grained and beautiful.
55. *Ratonia pyriformis,* Benth.—Diameter, 10 to 18 inches ; height, 30 to 45 feet. Moderate-sized tree ; timber firm and close-grained.
56. *Nephelium tomentosum,* F.M.—Diameter, 10 to 15 inches ; height 30 to 40 feet. Small-sized tree ; timber not used.
57. *Heterodendron diversifolium,* F.M.—4 to 6 inches ; height, 10 to 15 feet. Common in brigalow scrubs ; wood of a reddish colour ; its great strength renders it fit for pick-handles.
58. *Harpullia pendula,* Planch (Tulip-wood).—Diameter, 14 to 24 inches ; height, 50 to 60 feet. Found in some abundance on the alluvial banks of rivers. The timber is close-grained, firm, and beautifully marked, and much esteemed for cabinet-work.

ANACARDIACEÆ.

59. *Rhus rhodanthema,* F.M. (Dark Yellow-wood).—Diameter, 18 to 24 inches ; height, 50 to 70 feet. Tree of moderate size, of general occurrence on the banks of rivers ; the timber is soft, fine-grained, and beautifully marked, and is much esteemed for cabinet-work. The market value is from 100 to 120 shillings per thousand superficial feet.

RUBIACEÆ.

60. *Sarcocephalus cordatus,* Miq. (Leichhardt's Tree).—Diameter, 24 to 30 inches ; height, 40 to 60 feet. Moderate-sized tree, found on the Don River, Port Denison. Its wood is soft, close-grained, and takes a good polish ; often used for building and other purposes.
61. *Hodgkinsonia ovatiflora,* F.M.—Diameter, 6 to 10 inches ; height, 12 to 20 feet. Small tree ; timber close-grained.
62. *Canthium lucidum,* Hook and Arn.—Diameter, 6 to 12 inches ; height, 20 to 30 feet. Small tree ; wood hard and close-grained.

64. *Canthium oleifolium*, Hook.—Diameter, 5 to 10 inches ; height, 25 to 30 feet. In brigalow scrubs, near Ipswich ; wood hard, close-grained, and capable of a high polish.
65. *Canthium vacciniifolium*, F.M.—Diameter, 2 to 4 inches ; height, 6 to 10 feet ; wood close-grained.

MYRTACEÆ.

66. *Callistemon lanceolatus*, D.C. (Bottle Brush Tree).—Diameter 12 to 18 inches ; height, 30 to 40 feet. Small tree, growing in or near the beds of rivers, wood hard and heavy.
67. *Callistemon salignus*, D.C. (Broad-leaved Tea-tree).—Diameter, 18 to 24 inches ; height, 40 to 60 feet. Wood hard and close-grained, very durable underground.
68. *Melaleuca genistifolia*, Sm.—Diameter, 20 to 24 inches ; height, 30 to 40 feet. Moderate-sized tree, wood close-grained, hard, and durable.
69. *Melaleuca leucadendron*, Linn. (White Tea-tree).—Diameter 24 to 40 inches ; height, 40 to 60 feet. Moderate-sized tree, timber hard, and close-grained, excellent for posts in damp ground, and piles for wharves, and is said to be imperishable underground.
70. *Melaleuca styphelioides*, Sm. (Prickly-leaved Tea-tree).—Diameter, 24 to 30 inches ; height 40 to 60 feet. Moderate-sized tree, timber hard, close grained, stands well in damp situations. It has been said that this timber has never been known to decay.
71. *Melaleuca linariifolia*, Sm.—Diameter, 20 to 24 inches ; height, 30 to 40 feet. Moderate sized tree, timber hard, close, and durable.
72. *Melaleuca nodosa*, (Tea-tree).—Diameter, 10 to 20 inches ; height, 30 to 40 feet. Small tree, qualities same as Nos. 70 and 71.
73. *Angophora subvelutina*, F.M. (Apple Tree).—Diameter, 20 to 36 inches ; height, 40 to 60 feet. Occurring generally on rich forest lands ; timber strong and durable, much used by wheelwrights, also used for ship's timbers.
74. *Eucalyptus pilularis*, Sm. (Black-butt).—Diameter, 20 to 48 inches ; height, 60 to 80 feet. A large tree, furnishes excellent timber for house carpentry, or any purpose where strength and durability are required. Market value 80s. to 90s. per thousand.
75. *Eucalyptus hæmastoma*, Sm. (Spotted Gum).—Diameter 24 to 48 inches ; height, 60 to 120 feet. A very large tree, considered a first class timber for shipbuilding, and much used for wheelwright's work and other purposes. Market value, from 80s. to 90s. per thousand feet.
76. *Eucalyptus microcorys*, F.M.—Diameter, 18 to 36 inches ; height, 60 to 80 feet. A tall tree, occurring in the forest near the Brisbane River, timber strong and durable, used by wheelwrights for naves, felloes, and spokes.
77. *Eucalyptus hemiphloia*, F.M. (Yellow Box).—Diameter, 20 to 40 inches ; height, 50 to 75 feet. A moderate-sized tree, producing an excellent timber, famous for its hardness, toughness, and durability. Market value, from 80s. to 90s. per thousand feet.
78. *Eucalyptus siderophloia*, Benth. (Ironbark).—Diameter, 20 to 40 inches ; height, 70 to 100 feet. Occupant of many ridgy, stony, forest lands in East and West Moreton and Darling Downs districts. This timber has the highest reputation for strength and durability, and is used for large beams in building stores for heavy goods, railway sleepers, and other purposes where great strength is required. Market value, 80s. to 90s. per thousand.
79. *Eucalyptus melanophloia*, F. M. (Silver-leaved Ironbark).—Diameter, 18 to 24 inches ; Height, 30 to 70 feet.

80. *Eucalyptus maculata*, Hook (Spotted Gum).—Diameter, 20 to 36 inches; height, 60 to 80 feet. A very valuable timber, highly prized for many purposes on account of its strenght and elasticity, used for buggy-shafts, cogs of wheels, etc. In bridge-building it is used for members under tension, and is found to have the highest constant strength of any of the Queensland timbers.

81. *Eucalyptus saligna*, Sm. (Grey Gum).—Diameter, 24 to 40 inches; height, 60 to 90 feet. Large tree of frequent occurrence on the forest ridges near the Brisbane River. Useful timber, in good repute for building purposes, being both strong and durable. Market value, from 80s. to 90s. per thousand feet.

82. *Eucalyptus resinifera*, Sm. (Red Mahogany).— Diameter, 20 to 30 inches; height, 60 to 70 feet. The timber is much prized for its strength and durability, and is used for piles, as it is said to resist the action of cobra. Market value from 80s. to 90s. per thousand feet.

83. *Eucalyptus corymbosa*, Sm. (Bloodwood).—Diameter, 24 to 30 inches; height, 50 to 60 feet. A fair-sized tree, timber subject to gum-veins, but very durable, principally used for posts, does not readily take fire or suffer much from white ants. Market value, from 80 to 90 shillings per thousand feet.

84. *Eucalyptus botryoides*, Sm. (Blue Gum).—Diameter, 30 to 50 inches; height, 70 to 100 feet. Of frequent occurrence both upon the coast and in the interior; a valuable timber, hard, tough, and durable. The only timber used for felloes of wheels, and one of the finest timbers for ship-building. Market value, 80s. to 90s. per thousand feet.

85. *Eucalyptus terelicornis*, Sm. (Red Gum).—Diameter, 18 to 36 inches; height, 60 to 90 feet. A fair-sized tree; timber used in fencing, building, plough-beams, poles and shafts of drays, and also in ship-building. Market value from 80s. to 90s. per thousand feet.

86. *Eucalyptus Stuartiana*, F.M. (Turpentine tree).—Diameter, 24 to 40 inches; height, 60 to 90 feet; of common occurrence. Timber is hard and said to be exceedingly durable underground, and is difficult to burn; used for sleepers and many other purposes. Market value from 80s. to 90s. per thousand feet.

87. *Eucalyptus fibrosa*, F.M. (Stringybark).—Diameter, 18 to 36 inches; height, 40 to 75 feet. Timber much prized for flooring boards, and of considerable strength and durability. Market value from 80s. to 90s. per thousand feet.

88. *Eucalyptus tesselaris*, F.M. (Moreton Bay Ash).—Diameter, 14 to 24 inches; height, 30 to 60 feet. Timber of a brownish color, not hard, but tough; highly spoken of for building purposes in the northern parts of the colony. Market value from 80s. to 90s. per thousand feet.

89. *Eucalyptus melanophloia*, F.M. (Silver-leaved Ironbark).—Diameter, 18 to 24 inches; height, 30 to 60 feet. Small tree, timber used for fencing and other purposes. Market value from 80s. to 90s. per thousand feet.

90. *Eucalyptus platyphylla*, F.M.—Diameter, from 20 to 30 inches; height 60 to 80 feet. A moderate-sized tree; timber much used in house carpentery.

91. *Eucalyptus crebra*, F.M. (White narrow-leaved Ironbark).—Diameter, 20 to 36 inches; height, 70 to 90 feet. A fair-sized tree, producing an excellent timber—hard, tough, and durable; valuable for building purposes. Market value from 80s. to 90s. per thousand feet.

92. *Eucalyptus leptophleba*, F.M.—Diameter, 18 to 36 inches; height, 50 to 80 feet. Moderate-sized or large tree; timber hard and durable.

93. *Eucalyptus setosa*, Schau.—Diameter, 18 to 24 inches; height, 40 to 50 feet. A middle-sized tree; timber used for fencing.

94. *Eucalyptus terminalis*, F.M.—Diameter, 15 to 24 inches ; height, 40 to 50 feet. A small or middle-sized tree ; timber in good repute for posts, &c.

95. *Eucalyptus citriodora*, Hook. (Scented Gum).—Diameter, 18 to 34 inches; height, 50 to 80 feet. A good-sized tree ; timber hard and durable ; used for house carpentery.

96. *Eucalyptus melissiodora*, Lindl.—Diameter, 15 to 24 inches ; height, 40 to 60 feet. Small-sized tree ; timber tough and durable.

97. *Eucalyptus pellita*, F.M.—Diameter, 18 to 30 ; height, 50 to 70 feet. Moderate-sized tree ; timber used for flooring and other purposes.

98. *Tristania conferta*, R.B. (Box).—Diameter, 35 to 50 inches ; height, 80 to 100 feet ; very generally distributed on open forest ground. The timber is much prized for its strength and durable qualities. Market value from 80s. to 90s. per thousand feet. Used in ship-building ; ribs of vessels from this tree have lasted unimpaired thirty years and more.

99. *Tristania exiliflora*, F. M.—Small tree, timber not much used as yet.

100. *Tristania neriifolia*, R. B.—A small but handsome tree found along the banks of fresh-water streams ; timber very close and elastic ; used for carpenter's mallets and cogs of wheels in machinery.

101. *Backhousia myrtifolia*, Hook and Harv.—Diameter 12 to 18 inches, height 20 to 40 feet ; small tree, timber close-grained and prettily marked.

102. *Backhousia citriodora*, F. M.—Diameter 6 to 12 inches, height 20 to 30 feet ; small-sized tree, wood hard and fine-grained, useful for several purposes.

103. *Myrtus acmenioides*, F. M.—Diameter 12 to 18 inches, height 30 to 40 feet ; small tree, frequent in the scrubs ; timber close-grained, not much used.

104. *Myrtus Hillii*, Benth. (Scrub Ironwood).—Diameter 6 to 12 inches, height 20 to 40 feet ; small-sized tree, wood remarkably hard.

105. *Rhodamnia trinervia*, Blum.—Diameter 10 to 18 inches, height 20 to 30 feet ; small tree, wood close-grained and firm.

106. *Rhodomyrtus psidioides*, Benth.—Diameter 12 to 20 inches, height 30 to 40 feet ; frequent in the scrubs ; wood close-grained, not much known.

107. *Rhodamnia argentea*, Benth.—Diameter 15 to 22 inches, height 40 to 60 feet ; found in great abundance in moist low scrubs ; wood tough and firm.

108. *Myrtus Bidwillii*, Benth.—Diameter 6 to 10 inches, height 15 to 20 feet ; timber close-grained, not much known.

109. *Eugenia Ventenatii*, Benth.—Diameter 18 to 20, height 40 to 60 feet ; of frequent occurrence in moist scrubs ; wood close-grained and of a pinkish hue.

110. *Eugenia Smithii*, Poir. (Lilly Pillies).—Diameter 12 to 18 inches, height 30 to 40 feet ; wood close, but apt to split in seasoning.

111. *Eugenia grandis*, Wight.—Diameter 20 to 36 inches, height 40 to 70 feet ; a large and handsome tree ; timber close-grained, not much known.

112. *Eugenia angophoroides*, F. M.—Diameter 12 to 18 inches, height 30 to 40 feet ; small-sized tree ; timber but little known.

PROTEACEÆ.

113. *Grevillea robusta*, Cunn. (Silky Oak).—Diameter, 30 to 40 inches ; height, 80 to 100 feet. Of frequent occurrence in the scrubs along the coast and for a considerable distance in the interior. This timber is extensively used for staves for tallow casks, and is much in repute for cabinet-work. Market value from 90s. to 100s. per thousand feet

114. *Stenocarpus sinuatus*, Endl. (Tulip-tree).—Diameter, 18 to 30 inches; height, 40 to 80 feet. A moderate-sized tree; occurs often in scrubs some distance from the coast. Wood close-grained, hard, durable, and beautifully marked.

115. *Macadamia ternifolia*, F. M. (Queensland Nut).—Diameter, 3 to 12 inches; height, 30 to 50 feet. Small-sized tree; wood fine-grained and takes a good polish.

116. *Orites excelsa*, R. B.—Diameter, 6 to 14 inches; height, 30 to 40 feet. Of frequent occurrence in the scrubs bordering the coast. Timber hard, nicely marked, and takes a good polish.

117. *Banksia integrifolia*, Linn. (Beefwood).—Diameter, 8 to 12 inches; height, 20 to 30 feet. Occurring on sandy ridges near the coast and for a considerable distance into the interior.

118. *Persoonia lucida* (*var. latifolia*), Beck.—Diameter, 3 to 9 inches; height, 10 to 20 feet. Small-sized tree, found in sandy ridges on the coast. Wood prettily marked but not very durable.

119. *Banksia æmula*, R. B.—Diameter, 9 to 15 inches; height, 20 to 30 feet.

RHIZOPHOREÆ.

120. *Bruguiera Rheedii*, Blume. (Mangrove).—Diameter, 6 to 12 inches; height, 12 to 20 feet. Small tree; timber handsome; bark is astringent and used for tanning purposes.

SANTALACEÆ.

121. *Exocarpus latifolia*, Br. (Broad-leaved Cherry-tree).—Diameter, 6 to 9 inches; height, 15 to 25 feet. Small tree, of frequent occurrence in scrubs on the coast; the timber is very hard and fragrant; excellent for cabinet-work.

122. *Exocarpus cupressiformis*, Labill. (Cherry-tree).—Diameter, 4 to 8 inches; height, 10 to 16 feet. Small tree, found sparingly on open forest ground. The wood is close-grained and handsome.

MYOPORINEÆ.

123. *Eremophila Mitchelli*, Benth. (Bastard Sandalwood).—Diameter, 6 to 12 inches; height, 20 to 30 feet. Small tree, of frequent occurrence in open forest land in the Darling Downs District. Timber very hard, beautifully grained, and very fragrant; makes handsome veneers for cabinet-work.

124. *Myoporum acuminatum (Var parviflorum)*, R. B.—Diameter, 4 to 9 inches; height 12 to 15 feet. Timber soft and light.

125. *Myoporum platycarpum*, R.B.—Diameter, 12 to 15 inches; height, 15 to 25 feet. A small tree, wood close-grained, not used.

VERBENACEÆ.

126. *Avicennia officinalis*, Linn. (Mangrove).—Diameter, 19 to 24 inches; height, 20 to 30 feet. Found on salt water estuaries; timber used for knees of boats, stonemasons' mallets, etc.

127. *Gmelina Leichhardtii*, F.M. (Beech).—Diameter, 24 to 42 inches; height, 80 to 120 feet. Found in the scrubs bordering the rivers on the coast. A very useful timber, strong and durable, and easily worked; it does not expand by damp and contract by dry weather; much prized for the decks of vessels and the flooring of verandahs. Market value, from 120s. to 130s. per thousand feet.

128. *Vitex lignum-vitæ*, A. Cunn. (Lignum Vitæ).—Diameter, 20 to 24 inches; height, 50 to 70 feet. A tree of general occurrence in the moist low scrubs bordering the coast. The timber is hard, close grained, and of a brackish colour, used by cabinet-makers.

TILIACEÆ.

129 *Elæocarpus grandis,* F.M. (Callhoon).—Diameter, 24 to 36 inches; height, 80 to 100 feet. Frequent in low scrubs along the coast, timber soft and easily worked, used for boarding staves, etc.

LEGUMINOSÆ.

130 *Acacia falcata,* Willd.—Diameter, 6 to 12 inches; height, 20 to 30 feet. Small tree; wood hard, and much prized for making stockwhip handles.

131. *Acacia glaucescens,* Willd.—Diameter, 12 to 18 inches; height, 30 to 45 feet. Of frequent occurrence both in the scrubs and in open forest lands, wood close-grained, and prettily marked.

132. *Acacia Cunninghamii,* Hook.—Diameter, 9 to 12 inches; height, 20 to 30 feet. Small-sized tree, wood close-grained, and takes a good polish, found on the banks of the Brisbane.

133. *Acacia salicina,* Lindl.—Diameter, 6 to 12 inches; height, 30 to 40 feet. Found on scrubby land in the Darling Downs District; timber close-grained, and nicely marked.

133A. *Acacia implexa,* Benth.—Diameter, 12 to 16 inches; height, 30 to 40 feet. Small tree found on open forest ground, wood hard, and close-grained.

134. *Acacia harpophylla,* F. M.—Diameter, 12 to 20 inches; height 40 to 70 feet. A tall erect tree of general occurrence in the Rosewood scrubs. Timber hard, heavy and elastic, of a dark colour, giving a strong odour of violets.

135. *Acacia excelsa,* Benth. (Brigalow).—Diameter, 20 to 30 inches; height, 50 to 80 feet. This species covers immense tracks of rich scrub land, wood hard, close-grained, of a dark colour, used for building purposes, fencing, etc.

136. *Acacia doratoxylon,* A. Cunn.—Diameter, 6 to 12 inches; height, 20 to 35 feet. In scrubs and open forest ground, wood hard, and close-grained.

137. *Acacia decurrens (var. mollis.),* Lindl.—Diameter, 6 to 10 inches; height, 30 to 40 feet. This species is of very frequent occurrence through the Darling Downs.

138. *Acacia pendula,* A. Cunn (Weeping Myall).—Diameter, 6 to 12 inches; height, 20 to 35 feet. Small tree, well known for its violet scent, a small weeping tree, well known for its violet-scented wood, which is hard, close-grained, and beautifully marked; used by cabinet-makers and turners, in high repute for tobacco pipes.

139. *Acacia stenophylla,* A. Cunn (Ironwood).—Diameter, 15 to 24 inches; height 40 to 60 feet. On open forest ground on the Darling Downs. Timber is very hard, heavy, close-grained, dark, beautifully marked, and takes a fine polish.

140. *Acacia striata,* W. H.—Diameter, 6 to 18 inches; height 40 to 50 feet. Found on the Albert River; the trunk is beautifully streaked with green and white. The duramen is of a light-yellow colour, not unlike yellow-wood, but somewhat harder.

141. *Acacia penninervis,* Sieb.—Diameter, 2 to 4 inches; height, 6 to 12 feet. Scattered through open stony ridges.

142. *Barklya syringifolia,* F. M.—Diameter, 12 to 18 inches; height 40 to 60 feet. Found on fertile banks, and flats of rivers.

143. *Castanospermum australe,* A. Cunn (Moreton Bay Chestnut).—Diameter, 24 to 48 inches; height, 80 to 100 feet. A large tree of frequent occrruence on the banks of rivers. Timber is dark, and finely grained, not unlike walnut, used for cabinet-work, for which purpose it is well suited.

144. *Erythrina vespertilio,* Benth. (Coral-tree).—Diameter, 12 to 15 inches; height, 30 to 40 feet. Frequent both on the coast and in the interior; used by the natives for making shields.

144A. *Bauhinia Carronii,* F. M.—Diameter, 10 to 15 inches; height, 30 to 40 feet. A very handsome tree; timber used for furniture.

CORNACEÆ.

145. *Marlea vitiensis,* Benth. (Musk-tree).—Diameter, 6 to 12 inches; height 20 to 30 feet. Small tree, found in low, moist scrubs ; wood bright-yellow, with a fine undulating appearance, black in the centre.

JASMINEÆ.

146. *Olea paniculata,* R. B. (Native Olive).—Diameter, 18 to 24 inches; height, 50 to 70 feet. A moderate-sized tree, of frequent occurrence in the scrubs both on the coast and also in the interior. Timber close-grained, hard, and durable.

147. *Notelæa ovata,* R. B. (Dunga Vunga).—Diameter, 6 to 12 inches; height, 20 to 30 feet. Slender tree, found in scrubs; wood close-grained.

148. *Notelæa microcarpa,* R. B.—Diameter, 9 to 12 inches; height, 30 to 45 feet. Tree of frequent occurrence on the borders of scrubs on the coast; wood hard and close-grained.

LAURINEÆ.

149. *Endiandra pubens,* Meissn.—Diameter, 18 to 24 inches; height, 40 to 70 feet. Moderate-sized tree, of general occurrence in the scrubs on the banks of the Brisbane and Albert Rivers. Timber not as yet used.

150. *Tetranthera ferruginea,* R. B.—Diameter, 14 to 20 inches; height, 30 to 40 feet. Wood close-grained, not used.

151. See No. 176.

152. *Cryptocarya patentinervis,* F. M.—Diameter, 12 to 20 inches; height, 30 to 40 feet. A small-sized tree; timber of apparent value, but not used for any purpose.

EBENACEÆ.

153. *Cargillia australis,* R. B.—Diameter, 6 to 12 inches; height, 30 to 40 feet. Timber very tough and firm, and likely to be used for many purposes.

154. *Maba fasciculosa,* F. M.—Diameter, 18 to 24 inches; height, 60 to 80 feet. Of common occurrence in the scrubs bordering on river banks. Wood tolerably close-grained.

EUPHORBIACEÆ.

155. *Mallotus claoxyloides,* M. A.—Diameter, 9 to 16 inches; height, 15 to 30 feet. Occurring both in moist low scrubs and in dry rocky places. Timber white, hard, and close-grained.

156. *Mallotus philippinensis,* M. A.—Diameter, 6 to 14 inches; height, 30 to 45 feet. Small tree, generally found in rich scrubs. Wood close grained and very tough.

157. *Mallotus nesophilus,* F. Mu.—Diameter, 12 to 18 inches; height, 35 to 45 feet. Of frequent occurrence in low moist scrubs on the coast. Wood of a uniform white colour, soft, and easily worked.

158. *Petalostigma quadriloculare,* F. M. (Crab-tree.)—Diameter, 12 to 18 inches; height, 40 to 50 feet. Found in great abundance growing on poor sandy soil in the open forest. The timber is hard and fine-grained, and promises to be useful to the cabinet-makers.

158A. *Excæcaria agallocha,* Linn. (River Poisonous tree.)—Diameter, 6 to 18 inches; height, 20 to 30 feet. Found on the estuaries of saltwater creeks and rivers. Wood light, white, and soft.

159. *Briedelia exaltata,* F. M.—Diameter, 12 to 18 inches; height, 30 to 45 feet. Not unfrequent in moist low scrubs on the coast. Timber hard and close-grained.

160. *Dissiliaria baloghioides,* F. M. (Teak.)—Diameter, 18 to 30 inches ; height, 40 to 60 feet. Moderate-sized tree, found in great abundance on the coast scrubs. Timber hard, close-grained, and durable.

MONIMIACEÆ.

161. *Daphnandra micrantha,* Benth.—Diameter, 18 to 30 inches; height, 60 to 80 feet. Moderate-sized tree, occasionally found in low moist scrubs. Timber quite yellow when fresh, takes a fine polish, and is easily worked.

SAPOTACEÆ.

162. *Hormogyne cotinifolia,* D. C.—Diameter, 6 to 9 inches; height, 20 to 35 feet. Small tree, wood close-grained.
163. *Chrysophyllum pruniferum,* F. M.—Diameter, 12 to 20 inches; height, 30 to 70 feet. Moderate-sized tree, sparingly distributed over moist low scrubs. Wood of a uniform pale-yellow colour, close-grained.
163ᴀ. *Sersalisia sericea,* R. B.—Diameter, 8 to 12 inches; height, 20 to 40 feet. Small tree, frequent in moist scrubs. Timber hard and close-grained.
163ʙ. *Sersalisia obovata,* R. B.—Diameter, 8 to 12 inches; height, 20 to 35 feet. Small tree, frequent in low moist scrubs. Timber hard and close-grained.

APOCYNEÆ.

164. *Alstonia constricta,* F. M. (Fever Bark).—Diameter 6 to 20 inches, height 40 to 50 feet; of frequent occurrence in low moist scrubs, as well as in dry brigalow scrubs.

URTICEÆ.

165. *Celtis ingens,* F. M.—Diameter 6 to 12 inches, height 25 to 35 feet; small tree, frequent in the coast scrubs; wood white, soft, and pliable.
166. *Laportea photiniphylla,* Wedd. (Nettle-tree).—Diameter 15 to 24 inches, height 30 to 50 feet; wood soft and spongy.
167. *Morus calcar-galli,* Cunn. (Cockspur Thorn).—Heartwood, dark-yellow colour, used in dyeing.

ADDENDA.

170. *Brachychiton populneum,* R. B.
173. *Frenela Parlatorei,* F. M.—Diameter 20 to 36 inches, height 60 to 80 feet.
174. *Frenela Endlicheri,* Parlat.—Diameter 20 to 40 inches, height 60 to 100 feet.
175. *Casuarina suberosa,* Ott. et Diet.—Diameter 18 to 24 inches, height 40 to 50 feet.
176. *Litsœa dealbata,* Nees.—Diameter 18 to 24 inches, height 40 to 60 feet.

177ᴀ. Tulloch, W., Agricultural Reserve, Warwick—White Wheat; yield per acre, 25 bushels; weight per bushel, 68 lbs. 10 ozs.
177ʙ. McCulloch, A., Agricultural Reserve, Warwick—Wheat; yield per acre, 20 bushels; weight, 68 lbs. 8 ozs. per bushel.
177ᴄ. Free, A., Emu Creek, Warwick—Yield per acre, 20 bushels; weight, 68 lbs. 5½ ozs. per bushel.
177ᴅ. McPhee, J.—Malting Barley, Chevalier; yield per acre, 22 bushels; weight, 60 lbs. per bushel.
177ᴇ. Smith, J. Warwick—Malting Barley; yield per acre, 18 bushels; weight, 57 lbs. per bushel.
177ꜰ. Tulloch, W., Warwick—Cape Barley.
177ɢ. Strong, J., Brisbane—Maize.
177ʜ. Strong, J., Brisbane—Maize
177ɪ. Strong, J., Brisbane—Maize.
177ᴊ. Logan, W., Brisbane—Maize.
177ᴋ. Logan, W., Brisbane—Maize

COLLECTION OF VEGETABLE PRODUCTS ILLUS-
TRATIVE OF THE COLONY OF QUEENSLAND
BOTANIC GARDEN, BRISBANE, WALTER HILL,
COLONIAL BOTANIST AND DIRECTOR.

SUGARS.

ORDINARY COMMERCIAL SAMPLES TAKEN FROM BULK.

The production of sugar has now become a firmly established and increasing industry. In 1876, there were 13,690 acres under cultivation, and 70 mills and 12 distilleries employed in the manufacture of their produce. The cultivation of the sugar-cane in Queensland already extends over ten degrees of latitude, and upon our northern rivers there is still a boundless field for the successful prosecution of this remunerative industry.

BRISBANE DISTRICT—Lat. 27° 28′ S.; Lon. 153° 3′ E.

Average annual rainfall during 16 years, 52·26 inches, distributed over 127 days. Mean shade temperature, 70°·2 F. Mean maximum shade, 80′ F. Mean minimum, 59° F.

There are 17 sugar-mills in this district in connection with sugar estates, and there are also a large number of small growers, whose crops are either purchased by the mill-owners, or manufactured by them for the growers, at a percentage of the sugar obtained. There are also several distilleries in the district, which extends for a distance of 72 miles north and 18 miles south of the city of Brisbane. In some portions the frosts interfere with the cultivation of the sugar-cane. The geological formation consists of Devonian clay slates, shales, lepidodendron, and spinifer and conglomerates in the upper beds, crystalline limestone in the lower. Also, to the eastward, of paleozoic carboniferous formation, glossopteris, with productus spinifer, &c. The latitude and longitude given is always that of the chief town or port of the district.

1. *Coleridge Mills*, Brisbane River, W. Dart.—White sugar, vacuum pan; value, £31 10s. per ton.
2. *Coleridge Mills*, Brisbane River, W. Dart.—Counter, vacuum pan; value, £31 per ton.
3. *Oxley Creek*, Donaldson.—Counter; value, £33.
4. *Richmount*, Brisbane River, H. Berry.—Counter, open pan; value, £26.
4A. *Normanby Mill*, Owen Gardner.—Open pan; value, £25 10s.
4B. *Normanby Mill*, Owen Gardner.—Open pan; value, £23 10s.
4C. *Normanby Mill*, Owen Gardner.—Open pan; value, £23 10s.

LOGAN DISTRICT—Lat. 27° 28′ S.; Lon. 153° 8′ E.

Rainfall for 1875, 92·24 inches, distributed over 104 days. This district extends southward to the boundary of the colony of New South Wales, and includes the Albert, Pimpama, Coomera, and Nerang, all sugar-producing rivers. The land employed in the cultivation of sugar-cane consists principally of the rich alluvial flats bordering the abovementioned rivers. There is a large area of land under cultivation, and a considerable amount of capital has been invested in the erection of improved machinery. There are 18 mills in opera- tion. In the neighbourhood of the principal town, Beenleigh, the formation is mainly of sandstone alternating with schist and occasional patches of quartz. Coomera and Nerang are Devonian, consisting of clay slates, and shales, conglomerates in the upper beds, crystalline limestone in the lower.

5. *Ageston Plantation*, Logan River, W. H. Couldery.—Process of manufacture, ordinary three-roller mill, copper wall, and vacuum pan ; made from canes 18 months old, grown upon scrub soil ; value, £30.

6. *Ageston Plantation*—Logan River, W. H. Couldery.—Process of manufacture same as above ; value, £34.

7. *Ageston Plantation*, Logan River, W. H. Couldery.—Process of manufacture, same as Nos. 5 and 6 ; value, £32.

8. *Ageston Plantation*, Logan River, W. H. Couldery.—Made from cane growing upon low-lying forest soil ; process of manufacture same as Nos. 5, 6, and 7 ; this sample giving 1 lb. 2 oz. per gall. at 8° Baumé ; value, £32.

9. *Ageston Plantation*, Logan River, W. H. Couldery.—White sugar, vacuum pan ; value, £33.

10. *Ageston Plantation*, Logan River, W. H. Couldery. — Counter ; vacuum pan ; value, £29.

11. *Ageston Plantation*, Logan River, W. H. Couldery.—Ration sugar ; value £23 10s.

12. *Bannockburn*, Beenleigh, A. Watt.—Counter sugar, manufactured from Meera cane ; open pan and common lime process ; value £27.

13. *Bannockburn*, Beenleigh, A. Watt.—Molasses sugar ; open pan, lime, no patent used ; value £25.

14. *Benowa Plantation*, Nerang Creek, R. Muir.—Counter ; open pan direct from battery, no steam boiler ; value £31.

15. *Benowa Plantation*, Nerang Creek, R. Muir.—Ration sugar ; open pan direct from battery, no steam boiler ; value £23 10s.

16. *Binibi Plantation*, Nerang Creek, Philpott Brothers.—Counter sugar from first boiling of juice of ribbon cane, grown on scrub soil, fourth ratoons, yielding nearly two tons of sugar per acre ; the juice is tempered with lime, boiled in an open flat battery, and dried in a centrifugal ; value £29.

17. *Binibi Plantation*, Nerang, Philpott Brothers.—Ration sugar ; second boiling from juice of ribbon cane as above ; £26.

18. *Noyea Plantation*, Albert, Gartside, Muir, and Black.—Ration sugar ; open pan ; value £23 10s.

19. *Noyea Plantation*, Gartside, Muir, and Black.—Ration sugar ; open pan ; value, £24.

20. *Noyea Plantation*, Gartside, Muir, and Black.—Open pan ; value £29.

21. *Loganholme*, Logan River, W. Fryar.—Counter ; vacuum pan, concretor, and tray ; made from ribbon cane two years old ; value, £31.

22. *Loganholme*, Logan River, W. Fryar.—Counter ; made from ribbon cane ; concretor, tray, and vacuum pan ; value, £29.

23. *Otmoor*, Coomera, Bank of Queensland.—First sugar, manufactured from rappoo plant canes ten months old ; density, 9° Baumé ; yield, 1 lb. 6 ozs. per gallon ; ordinary lime process and open pan boiling ; value, £31.

24. *Otmoor*, Coomera, Bank of Queensland.—Second sugar, manufactured as the preceding ; value, £25.

25. *Tygum Plantation*, Logan, Lahey and Sons.—Counter ; open pan ; value, £31.

MARYBOROUGH DISTRICT.—Lat. 25° 35' S. ; Lon. 152° 43' E.

The average annual rainfall for three years was 61·31 inches, distributed over ninety-nine days. Sugar-cane is grown in large quantities in this district, which possesses twelve mills and a large sugar refinery at Yengarie. Many growers find it to their advantage to dispose of their juice, which is conveyed to Yengarie for manufacture. There are also several distilleries in the district. In the neighbourhood of Maryborough the formation is Devonian, consisting of clay, slate, and shale ; Tiaro—slate, coal, and sandstone ; Yengarie—coal formation; Bundaberg—alluvial deposits based upon conglomerate, the undisturbed formation is calcareous and carboniferous; Burnett—on the lower part of the river, serpentines, Devonian slates, limestone, and trap rocks.

26. *Kircubbin*, Maryborough, Lancelot Rawson.—Counter; open pan sugar; worked under Dr. Icery's mono-sulphite process; made from 12-months' old rappoc cane grown upon red soil.
27. *Nevada*, Maryborough, H. Monckton.—Counter; vacuum pan; made by Dr. Icery's mono-sulphite process; value, £33.
28. *Nevada*, Maryborough, H. Monckton.—Counter; vacuum pan; made by the ordinary lime process; value, £32.
29. *Yengarie Plantation*, Tooth and Cran.—White sugar; vacuum pan; passed through animal charcoal; value, £36
30. *Yengarie Plantation*, Tooth and Cran.—White sugar; vacuum pan; animal charcoal; value, £37 10s.
31. *Yengarie Plantation*, Tooth and Cran. — Raw sugar; vacuum pan; no animal charcoal used; £35.
32. *Burnett River*.—Ration; value, £27.
33. *Burnett River*, Shearon.—Counter; value, £32.
34. *Waterview*, Bundaberg, S. Johnston. — Counter; made from large yellow cane 2 years old, clarified and struck in the battery, yielding two tons per acre; value, £29.

MACKAY DISTRICT.—Lat. 21° 10′ S.; Long. 149° 5′ E.

Average annual rainfall for three years, 67·20 inches, during 84 days. This district, which from its great natural advantages has now become the most extensive sugar-producing district of the colony, is situated on the banks of the Pioneer River. There are already 18 mills and 4 distilleries in full work, and others in the course of erection. The suitability of the climate, coupled with the absence of frost and the presence of rich alluvial flats devoid of timber, have conduced to render this the most important sugar-producing district of Queensland. The south side of the Pioneer River is a rich alluvial plain extending 16 miles from east to west, by an average of 14 miles from north to south. The north side of the river is hilly, of volcanic origin, and in some places granite appears.

35. *Mackay*, Watts.—Counter; value £23 10s.
36. *Alexandra Plantation*, J. E. Davidson.—Produce this season about 570 tons; flat battery, Wetzell pan, lime process; value £27.
37. *Balmoral Plantation*, Hync and Co.—Produce this season about 350 tons; flat battery, Wetzell pan, lime process; value £27.
38. *Barrie Plantation*.—Produce this season about 250 tons; round battery, lime process; value £23 10s.
39. *Branscombe Plantation*, H. M. King.—Produce this season about 400 tons; round battery, Wetzell pan, sulphur and lime process; value £25.
40. *Cassada Plantation*.—Produce this season about 150 tons; flat battery, Wetzell pan, lime process; value £25.
41. *Cedars Plantation*.—Produce this season about 300 tons; round battery, Gadesden pans, lime process; value £25.
42. *Dumbleton Plantation*.—Produce this season about 250 tons; round battery, Wetzell pan, sulphur and lime process, value £26.
43. *Foulden Plantation*.—Produce this season, about 500 tons, round battery, vacuum pan, charcoal filters and lime; value, £33.
44. *Meadowlands Plantation*.—Produce about 700 tons; flat batteries, vacuum pan, mono-sulphite process; value, £31.
44A. *Meadowlands Plantation*.—Manufactured as No. 44; value, £33.
45. *Miclere Plantation*.—Produce this season about 250 tons; round battery, Wetzell pan, sulphur and lime process; value £31 10s.

46. *Nebia Plantation.*—Produce this season about 300 tons; round battery and lime process; value, £25 10s.
47. *Inverness Plantation.*—Produce this season about 150 tons; flat battery, Wetzell pan, and lime process; value £25
48. *Pleystowe Plantation.*—Produce this season about 400 tons; round battery, Bour pan, lime process; value, £25.
49. *Pioneer Plantation.*—Produce this season about 750 tons; round battery, vacuum pan, mono-sulphite process; value, £34.
50. *River Estate.*—Produce this season about   tons. Round batteries; vacuum pan; mono-sulphite process; value, £33.
51. *Te Kowai Plantation.*—Produce this season about 1,050 tons. Flat batteries; vacuum pan; lime process; no sulphur; value, £34.
52. *Te Kowai Plantation.*—First or best syrup sugar; value, £34.
53. *Te Kowai Plantation.*—Second or molasses sugar; value, £25. In the manufacture of Nos. 52 and 53, the usual lime process has been used, unassisted by filtering and bleaching agents. Vacuum pan. Total cost of production, including cultivation, not likely to exceed £9 per ton on the present crop, exclusive of interest on capital invested.
54. *Meadowlands Estate.*—First sugar; vacuum pan; value, £33.
55. *Meadowlands Estate.*—Second sugar; vacuum pan; value, £25.
56. *Meadowlands Estate.*—Third sugar; vacuum pan; value, £23 10s. Nos. 54, 55, and 56 are manufactured from black Java and rose bamboo canes. Cost of growing and manufacturing, £10 per ton.

HERBERT RIVER DISTRICT.—Lat. 18° 25′ S.; Lon. 146° 6′ E.

Average annual rainfall during three years, 104·15 inches, during 131 days. This comparatively new district possesses three sugar-mills, and with the large amount of superior land available, will most probably eventually become one of the most important sugar-producing districts of the colony. The geological formation consists of alluvial deposits over granite, surrounded by lofty ranges in the distance. The upper portion of the river is basaltic.

57. *Mackinade Plantation*, Neame and Co.—No. 1 sugar; value, £31.
58. *Mackinade Plantation*, Neame and Co.—No. 2 sugar; value, £30.
59. *Mackinade Plantation*, Neame and Co.—No. 3 sugar, value, £29. In the manufacture of the above three sugars, the vacuum pan was used, but no filtration. The yield per acre has reached as high as three tons, but the average may be stated at fully two tons.

FARINAS.

WHEATEN FLOUR AND MEAL (TRITICUM SATIVUM – LAWSON).

In the year 1876, there were five flour mills in operation in the colony, in the towns of Warwick, Allora, and Toowoomba, and the quantity of grain passed through their hands was, wheat 102,200 bushels, and maize, 11,240 bushels.

61. *Hayes and Co., Warwick.*—Wheaten flour from wheat grown in the district. Lat. 28° 12′ S.; lon. 152° 16′.
62. *Kates and Co., Allora.*—Wheaten Flour, from wheat grown in the district. Lat. 28° 2′ S.; lon., 152° 2′ E.
62A. *Wursching, C.*—Rye Flour, from rye grown in the district.
63. *Hayes and Co., Warwick.*—Wheaten Meal, from wheat grown in the district.
64. *Hon. W. Pettigrew, Brisbane.*—Wheaten Meal.

MAIZE MEAL.

65. *Hon. W. Pettigrew.*—Maize Meal (Zea Mays, Linn). grown in the district. Lat. 27° 28′ S.; lon. 153° 3′ E.

ARROWROOT.

Arrowroot is cultivated with success in various portions of the colony; the supply has for some years exceeded the local demand, and the surplus is exported to the southern colonies. There are 30 manufactories, 27 of which are in the Logan district. In 1876, 293,670 lbs. were produced, of which 162,495 lbs. were exported valued at £3,350. This does not represent the total produce of the area under crop, as in many instances it is used as pig-food. First-class samples can be purchased in quantity at from twopence to threepence per lb.

66. *Thomas Sharrocks, Bundaberg.*—Lat. 24° 50′ S.; lon. 152° 25′ E.—West Indian Arrowroot (Maranta arundinacea, Lin.), yield 2½ tons per acre.
67. *Botanic Garden, Brisbane.*—East Indian Arrowroot (Canna edulis, Ker.).
68. *Botanic Garden, Brisbane.*—West Indian Arrowroot (Maranta arundinacea, Linn.).
69. *G. Hall, Carlton Farm, North Pine River.*—West Indian Arrowroot (Maranta arundinacea, Linn.).
70. *Lahey and Sons, Tygum, Logan River.*—West Indian Arrowroot (Maranta arundinacea, Linn.).
71. *J. Mills, Pimpama,* West Indian Arrowroot (Maranta arundinacea, Linn.)
72. *Botanic Garden, Brisbane.*—Ground Rice (Oryza sativa, Linn.).
73. *Botanic Garden, Brisbane,* Cassava sweet (Manihot Janipha, Pohl.).
74. *Botanic Garden, Brisbane.*—Cassava bitter (Manihot utilissima, Pohl.).
75. *Botanic Garden, Brisbane.*—Zamia Flour, prepared from Macrozamia spiralis, Miq., used as an article of food by the natives.
76. *J. Burnett, Burpengary.*—East Indian Arrowroot (Canna edulis, Ker.).
77. *J. Burnett, Burpengary.*—West India arrowroot (Maranta arundinacea—Linn.).
78. *J. Burnett, Burpengary.*—Tapioca (Manihot utilissima—Pohl.)

CEREALS.

The principal wheat-growing districts are in the neighbourhood of Toowoomba, Warwick, and Allora, situated on the Darling Downs, at an elevation of 2,000 feet above the level of the sea. Maize is also largely cultivated, more especially upon the rich alluvial lands on the tidal rivers. The Statistical Report for 1876 gives the area under wheat as 5,967 acres, of which 1,165 were affected with rust and 347 entirely unproductive from the same cause. The total yield from the clean crops was 91,170 bhls., giving an average of 20 bhls. 28 lbs., although in some districts the average was as high as 28 bhls. 4 lbs.

WHEAT (TRITICUM SATIVUM—LAWSON).

79. *C. Armstrong, Warwick.*—Talavera wheat.
80. *Geo. Bell, Bundaberg.*—Wheat—yield, 36 bhls. per acre.
81. *James Hood, Bundaberg.*—Yield, 35 bhls.
82. *C. and S. Hayes, Warwick.*—Wheat.
83. *Walker, R. F., Toowoomba.*—White Tuscan.
84. *Walker, R. F., Toowoomba.*—White Lammas.
85. *Walker R. F., Toowoomba.*—White wheat.
86. *Price W., Bundaberg.*—Yield, 52 bushels.

MAIZE (ZEA MAYS—LINN.).

This crop is very extensively cultivated upon the rich scrub lands coast, and the yield varies from 40 to 120 bushels per acre according and climate. The area under crop in 1876 was 41,705 acres.

87. *Ferguson, W., Coomera.*—White maize ; cost of cultivation, £3 per acre ; yield, 80 bushels per acre—considered a valuable variety.
88. *Ferguson W., Coomera.*—Red maize ; cost of cultivation, £3 per acre ; yield, 75 bushels.
89. *Frankland H., Upper Albert.*—Maize from a crop of 30 acres grown upon rich forest soil, planted in November, and matured with little or no rain.
90. *Hall, G., Carlton Farm, North Pine.*—Maize.
91. *Hall, G., Carlton Farm, North Pine.*—Maize.
92. *Walker, R. F., Toowoomba.*—Yellow flint maize.
93. *Walker, R. F., Toowoomba.*—Malting barley.
94. *Walker, R. F., Toowoomba.*—Oats.
95. *Botanic Garden, Brisbane.*—Upland rice (Oryza sativa—Linn.)
96. *Botanic Garden, Brisbane.*—Upland rice (Oryza sativa—Linn.)
97. *Botanic Garden, Brisbane.*—Upland rice (Oryza sativa—Linn.)
98. *Botanic Garden, Brisbane.*—Upland rice (Oryza sativa—Linn.)
99. *Botanic Garden, Brisbane.*—Upland rice (Oryza sativa—Linn.)
100. *Botanic Garden, Brisbane.*—Upland rice (Oryza sativa—Linn.)

TEA, COFFEE, SPICES, ETC.

Both tea and coffee can be successfully cultivated in Queensland. In the southern portion of the colony the coffee-plant arrives at maturity in six or seven years, on the northern rivers it commences bearing at two years old ; although in the southern districts the yield is good, the northern districts, more especially the sheltered ridges of the Herbert, Daintree, Mossman, and Endeavour Rivers, are found more suitable to its profitable cultivation. Tea grows luxuriantly on the coast, but this plant, in order to develop the full flavour of the leaf, requires a period of rest that cannot be obtained where warmth and consequent stimulus to growth is always present, and a higher elevation, such as the Darling Downs, is found more suitable to this plant. Paraguay tea is admirably adapted for cultivation in many parts of the colony, and affords a heavy yield. In the more northern districts, Theobroma Cacao, together with nutmeg, cinnamon, cloves, and other spice-bearing plants, give great promise of future success.

101. *Botanic Garden, Brisbane*, Lat. 27° 28′ S. ; lon. 153° 6′ E.—Black Tea (Thea Bohea, Linn.).
101A. *Botanic Garden, Brisbane.*—Tea (Thea Bohea, Linn.)
102. *Botanic Garden, Brisbane.*—Coffee leaves (Coffea arabica, Linn.) ; prepared as tea.
103. *Botanic Garden, Brisbane.*—Paraguay Tea (Ilex Paraguariensis, St. Hil.).
103A. *Botanic Garden, Brisbane.*—Paraguay Tea or Maté (Ilex Paraguariensis, St. Hil.).
104. *Sandrock, G. R., Bowen*, Lat. 20° 1′ S. ; lon. 148° 16′ E.—Coffee (Coffea arabica, Linn.).
105. *Botanic Garden.*—Coffee (Coffea arabica, Linn.).
106. *Stewart, J., Herbert River*, Lat. 18° 25′ S. ; lon. 146° 6 E.′—Coffee (Coffea arabica, Linn.).
107. *Stewart, J., Gairloch, Herbert River.*—Coffee, pea berry (Coffea arabica, Linn.).
108. *Williams, A., Logan Road.*—Coffee beans, this season's growth (Coffea arabica, Linn.).
109. *Williams, A., Logan Road.*—Coffee beans, last season's growth (Coffea arabica, Linn.).
110. *Botanic Garden.*—Senna (Cassia acutifolia, Delil.).
111. *Botanic Garden.*—Senna (Cassia acutifolia, Delil.).
112. *Botanic Garden.*—Rosella, dried (Hibiscus sabdariffa, Lin.). Prepared in this manner the flavour is retained for a number of years,

113. *Botanic Garden.*—Bananas, dried (Musa paradisiaca, Linn.). When coarsely ground and sifted, this forms a farina much esteemed in South America, known in British Guiana as "conquin tay."
114. *Botanic Garden.*—Bunya Bunya nuts (Araucaria Bidwillii, Hook). Used as an article of food by the natives, who cut large quantities of it after roasting at a fire.
115. *Botanic Garden.*—Queensland nut (Macadamia ternifolia, F. M.).
116. *Botanic Garden.*—Queensland nut (Macadamia ternifolia, F. M.).
117. *Botanic Garden.*—Cycas media, R. B. Used as an article of food by the natives ; an excellent farina is prepared from it.
118. *Williams, A., Logan Road.*—Cinnamon (Laurus cinnamomum, Lin.).
119. *Botanic Garden.*—Cayenne Pepper (Capsicum baccatum, Linn.)—Bird's eye.
120. *Botanic Garden.*—Cayenne Pepper (Capsicum grossum, Willd.)—Béll Pepper.
121. *Botanic Garden.*—Cayenne Pepper (Capsicum annuum, Linn.)—Spanish Pepper.
122. *Botanic Garden.*—Specimens of silk.

DYEING MATERIALS.

The climate and soil of many portions of the colony are well suited to the production of madder and indigo of superior quality. In addition to these, many of our indigenous plants, amongst others Pipturus propinquus, Morus calcar-galli, Laportea gigas, etc., possess valuable dyeing properties.

123. *Botanic Garden.*—Madder (Rubia tinctorum, Lin.).
124. *Botanic Garden.*—Logwood (Hœmatoxylon campechianum, Lin.).
125. *Botanic Garden.*—Cockspur Thorn (Morus calcar-galli, A. Cunn.).
126. *Botanic Garden.*—Turmeric (Curcuma longa, Linn.).
127. *Botanic Garden.*—Indigo (Indigofera tinctoria, Linn.).

FIBRES.

Although Queensland is rich in indigenous fibre-yielding plants, none of them as yet, with the exception of Sida retusa (Queensland hemp) have been brought prominently into notice. Almost the whole of the recognized commercial fibres can be grown with success, and the attention of many of our cultivators is being drawn to their production.

128. *Botanic Garden.*—Jute (Corchorus capsularis, Linn.)
128A. *Botanic Garden.*—Jute (Corchorus capsularis, Linn.)
129. *Botanic Garden.*—Jute (Corchorus olitorius, Linn.)
129A. *Botanic Garden.*—Jute (Corchorus olitorius, Linn.)
130. *Botanic Garden.*—Rosella Hemp (Hibiscus subdariffa, Linn.)
131. *Botanic Garden.*—Rosella Hemp (Hibiscus sabdariffa, Linn.)
132. *Botanic Garden.*—Sunn Hemp (Crotalaria juncea, Linn.)
133. *Botanic Garden.*—Pita Hemp (Agave americana, Linn.)
134. *Botanic Garden.*—Mexican Hemp (Fourcroya gigantea, Vent.)
135. *Botanic Garden.*—(Hibiscus mutabilis, Linn.)
136. *Botanic Garden.*—White Mulberry (Morus alba, L.)
137. *Botanic Garden.*—Queensland Hemp (Sida retusa, Linn.)
138A. *Botanic Garden.*—Queensland Hemp (Sida retusa, Linn.)
139. *Botanic Garden.*—Queensland Hemp (Sida retusa, Linn.)
140. *Botanic Garden.*—Vacoa or Screw Pine (Pandanus utilis, Bojer.) Fibre made from aerial roots.
Botanic Garden.—Agave, Sp.
142. *Botanic Garden.*—Adam's Needle Fibre (Yucca gloriosa, Willd.)
143. *Botanic Garden.*—Silk Grass Fibre (Yucca aloifolia, Lin.)
144. *Botanic Garden.*—(Dracœna Draco Lin.)
145. *Botanic Garden.*—Cuba Bast (Paritium elatum, Don.)

146. *Botanic Garden.*—Bowstring Hemp (Sanseviera Zeylanica, Willd.)
147. *Botanic Garden.*—Vacoa or Screw Pine (Pandanus utilis, Bojer.)
148. *Botanic Garden.*—Flax (Linum usitatissimum, Linn.)
149. *Botanic Garden.*—New Zealand Flax (Phormium tenax, Forst.)
150. *Botanic Garden.*—Cordage made from (Linum usitatissimum, Linn.)
150A. *Botanic Garden.*—Cordage made from Queensland Hemp (Sida retusa, Lin.)
150B. *Botanic Garden.*—Short staple cotton (Gossypium herbaceum, Linn.)
150C. *Botanic Garden.*—Brisbane short staple cotton (Gossypum herbaceum, Lin).

ESSENTIAL OILS, TINCTURES, Etc., (Prepared by L. Carmichael, Chemist.

The myrtaceous trees and shrubs, which are found in immense quantities throughout Australia, are all, without exception, characterised by the presence of essential oils in greater or lesser quantities. This is not only the case with the Eucalypti, but also with species of Melaleuca, Leptospermum, and various others. Many of the Acacias produce flowers, from which agreeable perfumes can be obtained. As yet this branch of industry can hardly be said to have proceeded beyond the experimental stage, although it will no doubt receive an impetus from the discovery of a new species of Eucalyptus in Northern Queensland, from which Mr. K. T. Staiger, F.L.S., has obtained an oil possessing superior properties.

151. *Botanic Garden*—Oil of Blue Gum (Eucalyptus botryoides, Sm.). Therapeutic uses, antiseptic, useful in putrid fevers and fœtid suppurations.
152. *Botanic Garden.*—Tincture of Crab-tree (Petalostigma quadriloculare, F. M.). Contains a very powerful bitter, and is said to possess the same properties as Peruvian Bark.
153. *Botanic Garden.*—Essence of Verbena, scented Ironbark from the Palmer River (Eucalyptus, Sp.). This is obtained from a recently discovered Eucalyptus not yet named, possessing the most powerful and agreeable perfume that has yet been obtained from any of the Myrtaceæ.
154. *Botanic Garden.*—Tincture of Red Gum (Eucalyptus tereticornis,Sm.), Darling Downs. Possessing valuable therapeutic properties.
155. *Botanic Garden.*—Essence of Jasmine (Jasminum grandiflorum, Linn.)
156. *Botanic Garden.*—Essence of Acacia (Acacia farnesiana, Willd). A native of the warmer parts of Australia ; found as far south as the Darling River. Its scented flowers are much sought after for perfumery.
157. *Botanic Garden.*—Oil of Orange (Citrus aurantium, Linn.)
158. *Botanic Garden.*—Tincture of Gelsemium, as prescribed by Dr. Cannan, Brisbane ; a plant of therapeutical importance, the active principle of which is gelseminin, said to be useful in cases of neuralgia. Obtained from (Gelsemium nitidum—Mich.)
159. *Botanic Garden.*—Tincture of Bitter Bark (Alstonia constricta, F.M.) This tree is of frequent occurrence in the scrubs ; the bark is thick, of a yellow colour, deeply fissured and of intense bitterness, and is reputed to possess the same properties as quinine : is used in cases of fever and ague with good effect.
160. *Botanic Garden.*—Orange Bitters (Citrus Bigaradia—Duhl.)
161. *Botanic Garden.*—Hyapana Bitters (Eupatorium Ayapana—Vent.), used as a stimulant, tonic, and diaphoretic. It contains eupatorin and much essential oil peculiar to the plant ; it is also used in the form of infusion in dyspepsia and affections of the bowels.
162. *Botanic Garden.*—Liquid anotto, (Bixa Orellana, Linn.)
164. *Botanic Garden.*—Quassia (Quassia amara, Linn.)

165. *Botanic Garden.*—Tamarinds (Tamarindus indicus, Linn.)
166. *Botanic Garden.*—Dugong Oil obtained from Halicore Australis, used by many medical practitioners instead of cod-liver oil, being considered to possess the same therapeutic qualities, combined with a more agreeable taste.
167. *Botanic Garden.*—Castor Oil (Ricinus communis, Linn.)
168. *Botanic Garden.*—Ipecacuanha (Cephaëlis Ipecacuanha, Rich.)
169. *Botanic Garden.*—Croton Oil (Croton Tiglium, Linn.)
170. *Botanic Garden.*—Oil of Lemon, scented gum (Eucalyptus citriodora Hook). The dried leaves of this species preserve books and clothes, from the attacks of insects, and at the same time impart an agreeable perfume. The leaves used as a pillow are reputed to afford immunity from fever and ague.
170A. *Botanic Garden.*—Pitcheri. Used by the blacks; when chewed produces excitement and intoxication. Perfect specimens not yet obtained.

GUM RESINS.

171. *Botanic Garden.*—Cypress Pine Gum (Callitris columellaris F. M.) The similarity of the exudation from this tree with that of the Mediterranean sandrac pine is apparent.
172. *Botanic Garden.*—Bloodwood Gum (Eucalyptus corymbosa, Sm.) This gum can be easily obtained in quantity. In common with other Eucalyptus gums it possess valuable tanning properties. With the assistance of this gum resin, the photographs illustrative of Queensland were taken by Mr. R. Daintree whilst travelling.
173. *Botanic Garden.*—Bunya Bunya Gum (Araucaria Bidwilli, Hook.)
174. *Botanic Garden.*—Catechu from (Eucalyptus fibrosa, F.M.) powerful astringent, and in domestic medicine is frequently employ in cases of diarrhœa.
175. *Botanic Garden.*—Grass-tree Gum (Xanthorrhœa arborea, R. B.) From the balsamic resin of this plant, which is in many respects similar, if not identical, with benzoin, a fragrant spirituous varnish can be prepared. This resin has been used for fumigation and in the preparation of sealing-wax. It has also been employed as a nankin dye for calico.
176. *Botanic Garden.*—Bottle-tree Gum (Sterculia rupestris, Benth.) This gum, which has somewhat the appearance of Tragacanth, exudes from the tree in large quantities.

BARKS, MEDICINAL AND TANNING.

177. *Botanic Garden.*—Bark of the Blue Gum (Eucalyptus botryoides, Sm.) Used in domestic medicine, in cases of dysentery, with beneficial effect.
178. *Botanic Garden.*—Bark of Ironbark (Eucalyptus siderophloia, Benth.) Very generally used by tanners, and considered one of the best barks for that purpose. Can be obtained in quantity.
179. *Botanic Garden.*—Mangrove Bark (Bruguiera Rheedii, Blume.) This bark is astringent and used for tanning purposes.
180. *Botanic Garden.*—Green Wattle Bark (Acacia mollissima, Willd.) Bark used for tanning purposes.
181. *Botanic Garden.*—Black Wattle Bark (Acacia decurrens, Willd.) This species is of frequent occurrence, and is much prized for tanning. The quantity of tannin contained in dry bark varies from 18 to 33 per cent.
182. *Botanic Garden.*—Fever Bark (Alstonia constricta, F.M.), described at No. 159.
183. *Botanic Garden.*—Crab-tree Bark (Petalostigma quadriloculare, F.M.). See No. 170.

SPIRITS.

183. *W. H. Couldery, Ageston.*—Rum.
185. *Normanby Distillery,* Owen Gardner.—Rum, 30·7 o.p. ; value, 2s. 4d. per gallon.
186. *Normanby Distillery,* O. Gardner.—Rum, set up with pine-apple juice, 34 o.p. ; value, 2s. 5s. per gallon.
187. *Normanby Distillery,* O. Gardner.—Rum, 30·70 o.p. ; value, 2s. 4d. per gallon.
188. *Normanby Distillery,* O. Gardner.—Rum, 26·30 o p. ; value, 2s. 4d. per gallon.
189. *Normanby Distillery,* O. Gardner.—Rum, set up with pine-apple juice, 34 o.p. ; value, 2s. 5d. per gallon.
190. *Normanby Distillery,* O. Gardner.—Rum, 26·30 o.p. ; value, 2s. 4d. per gallon.

N.B.—The above strengths are all taken with Sykes' hydrometer.

MISCELLANEOUS.

191. *Botanic Garden.*—Midgeen canes, in the rough, one prepared specimen, (Areca monostachya, R. B.) ; value, 1s. per dozen.
191A. *Botanic Garden.*—Midgeen cane from Bellenden Kerr, Northern Australia (Areca minor, W. Hill.)
192. *Botanic Garden.*—Cardwell cane, rough cane, one prepared specimen (Flagellaria indica, Linn)
194. *Botanic Garden.*—Mackay bean (Entada scandens, Roxb.)
195. *Hall, S., Carlton Farm.*—Bottle of Lime-juice, made from Citrus Limetta, Risso, from which the best lime-juice is obtained.
196. *Egg-stand and Cups*—manufactured from Queensland timbers :—

    Cup No. 1—Musk Wood (Marlea vitiensis, Benth.)
           „   2—Native Olive (Olea paniculata, R. B.)
           „   3—Silky Oak—Grevillea robusta, A. Cunn.)
           „   4—Satin Wood (Xanthoxylon brachyacanthum, F. M.)
           „   5—Native Lime (Citrus australasica, F. M.)
           „   6—Native Orange (Citrus australis, Planch)
           „   7—Swamp Oak (Casuarina equisetifolia, Forst.)
           „   8—Forest Oak (Casuarina torulosa, Ait.)
           „   9—Rosewood (Acacia excelsa, Benth.)
           „   10—Red Cedar (Cedrela Toona, Roxb.)
           „   11—Weeping Myall (Acacia pendula, A. Cunn.)
           „   12—Moreton Bay Chestnut (Castanospermum australe, A. Cunn.)
    Sole of Stand 15—Beech (Gmelina Leichhardtii, F. M.)
    Pillar of do. 16—Cypress Pine (Callitris columellaris, F. M.)
    Spoon Rack 17—Ironwood (Acacia stenopnylla, A. Cunn.)
    Salt Cup 18—Deep Yellow Wood (Rhus rhodanthema, F. M.)
197. *Bitter Cups* 13—Crab Tree (Petalostigma quadriloculare, F. M.)
                   14—Bitter Bark (Alstonia constricta, F. M.)

TOBACCO.

Although tobacco has been cultivated for a considerable period, owing to the general want of experience and skill on the part of the growers, the quality of the product was not as good as could be desired. Within the last few years, aided by enlarged experience, this difficulty has been overcome, and an improved quality of leaf produced. Tobacco culture when skillfully conducted has proved itself a very profitable occupation. All the principal American varieties are cultivated and the cultivation of the newer and more esteemed descriptions as Shiraz, Nicotiana persica, and varieties from Bhilsa, and Ispahan, is now becoming general. The unusually unfavourable season that we have just experienced, has materially affected the tobacco crop, and consequently the exhibits are not so numerous as they otherwise would have been.

198. *Soegaard H., Nindooinbah.*—Manufactured Tobacco, Plug.
199. *Soegaard H., Nindooinbah.*—Cigars.
200. *Soegaard H., Nindooinbah*—Manufactured Tobacco, Twist.
201. *Soegaard H., Nindooinbah.*—Cigars.
202. *Nerang Creek.*—Kentucky Leaf.
203. *Ipswich Reserve.*—Alabama Leaf, Cigar Tobacco.
204. *Albert River.*—Virginia Leaf.
205. *Pine River.*—Connecticut Leaf.
206. *Coomera River*, W. Ferguson.—2 samples of Leaf Tobacco.
207. *Mahony, J. Cunnungera Creek.*—6 samples of Leaf Tobacco.

SPECIMENS OF INDIGENOUS PASTURE GRASSES AND FODDER PLANTS.

208. *Andropogon annulatus*, Forsk. (Blue Grass.)—An excellent summer grass of an upright habit of growth, good pasture, but is not very productive during the winter months.
209. *Andropogon acicularis*, Retz.—Strong growing grass; suitable for cattle, and eaten freely by them ; found throughout Queensland, but is most plentiful in the northern district.
210. *Andropogon erianthoides*, F. M.—Found on the Darling Downs. It is a very superior grass, and stock are considered to thrive better upon it than upon most other grasses. It produces a heavy crop of rich succulent herbage, much relished by all descriptions of stock. It spreads from the roots and also seeds freely.
211. *Andropogon Gryllus*, Linn.—An excellent pasture grass, easily recognized by its golden beard. It produces a large quantity of feed during the summer months, and is met with throughout Queensland, generally upon high land.
212. *Andropogon ha'epensis*, Sib.—Tall growing perennial grass, valuable for both hay and pasture. It an excellent cattle grass, though not much sought after by sheep. In the northern districts it grows strong and succulent, resembling a cultivated sorghum. There are several varieties of this fine grass.
213. *Andropogon montanus*, Roxb.—A tall, strong-growing, coarse grass, deep rooted, and of stoloniferous habit, found on the Darling Downs, and is partial to rich flats. The flower panicles possess a peculiar perfume.
214. *Andropogon nervosus*, Rott.—(Rat-tail grass.) An upright growing grass, found throughout the colony, rather coarse, but yields a fair amount of feed which is readily eaten by cattle.
215. *Andropogon pertusus*, Willd.—Good pasture grass, very generally distributed, stands drought well and is a fair winter grass if the weather is not too severe. It may be recognized by the little pit upon the glume.
216. *Andropogon refractus*, R. B. (Kangaroo Grass.)—An excellent grass for either pasture or hay, common in open country in the southern parts of the colony. It is a very productive summer grass, but makes little growth during the winter unless upon sheltered forest land. Its roots have a strong aromatic flavour.
217. *Andropogon rottboelloides*, Steud.—A large grass found on the rivers of northern Queensland. Its culm rises to the height of eight feet. It yields a large quantity of fodder, as its culm, seed, and foliage, together with the base of its thick stem, are eagerly eaten by cattle and horses,

218. *Andropogon triticeus*, R. B.—A robust perennial, and one of the tallest of our tropical grasses. The flower-stalks attain a height of nine feet, and are hard and cane-like; but a quantity of leafy feed is produced at their bases. Its strong and wiry roots penetrate from two to three feet into the ground. Cattle and horses are extremely fond of this grass.

219. *Agrostis Solandri*, F. M.—Perennial and annual. Found in almost all parts of Australia: plentiful on the Darling Downs, where it prefers the strongest wet land. It is one of the first grasses to spring after rains, and affords a supply of nutritious herbage until dried up by the summer heat. An excellent winter grass, and the herbage is sweet and succulent.

220. *Anthistiria australis*, R. B.—(Common kangaroo grass.) A tall perennial upright growing grass, often three feet in height. The roots are strong, fibrous, and penetrating. It is found in all parts of Australia, forms but few perfect seeds, and these do not germinate freely. It is one of the finest and most useful of the indigenous grasses. It remains green during the summer, but turns a little brown in the autumn, when its nutritive qualities are at the highest. Horses keep in better condition on this grass, doing hard work, than on almost any other species of native grass.

221. *Anthistiria avenacea*, F. M.—(Darling Downs.) Oat grass, one of the most productive grasses in Australia, and unlike other kangaroo grasses, it possesses the advantage of being a prolific seeder.

222. *Anthistiria ciliata*, L.—Kangaroo grass of Northern Queensland. This is an excellent grass for stock, and makes a larger amount of bottom feed than the other kangaroo grasses.

223. *Anthistiria membranacea*, Lindl. (Barcoo Grass.)—One of the best pasture grasses in Queensland. This grass is exceedingly brittle when dry, stock are found licking the broken parts from the ground.

224. *Arundinella nepalensis*, Trin.—A grass well adapted for hay. On the Darling Downs under cultivation has been cut three times during the season.

225. *Chloris divaricata*, R. B. (Dog-tooth Star Grass.)—An early grower, and although the stalks appear dry, yields a quantity of nutritious feed.

226. *Chloris ventricosa*, R. B. (Blue Star Grass.)—An erect quick growing species, found along the borders of scrubs, and produces a large quantity of leafy feed.

227. *Chloris scariosa*, F. M.—Particularly handsome grass, and excellent pasture; found in the northern and western districts.

228. *Cynodon Dactylon*, Pers. (Couch or Indian Doub Grass.)—This is generally considered an introduced grass, but is indigenous to Northern Australia. It is found throughout the colony, and is a good pasture grass, especially when mixed with white clover.

229. *Danthonia pectinata*, Lindl. (Mitchell Grass.)—This is a valuable perennial desert grass, resisting drought, and sought with avidity by stock.

230. *Danthonia lappacea*, Lindl.—This grass, although of rather a coarser nature than the preceding one, possesses the same characteristics, and from the well-known fattening and drought-resisting qualities of both species, they are deserving of cultivation. Seed has been sent to America, for trial in the Southern States.

231. *Eleusine indica*, Gœrt.—In the southern districts this is a strong succulent pasture grass in summer; but further north it affords good pasture throughout the season, and may be recognized by its deep green colour, strong stalks, and star-like panicle, the spikelets of which are flat and broad.

232. *Festuca Billardierii*, Steud.—Perennial grass ; grows about two feet in height, does not perfect its seed well, produces plenty of tender foliage, and is not much affected by dry seasons, or easily injured by overstocking. It is a valuable grass, and may be considered one of the best of our winter grasses.

233. *Helopus annulatus*, Nees (Early Spring Grass).—This grass stands well during the winter months, makes early spring growth, and is valuable as a species yielding feed throughout the year.

234. *Imperata arundinacea*, Cyr. (Blady Grass).—This is one of the grasses most frequently met with on rich alluvial land, and is one of the most common grasses of the North, and produces after being burnt a large quantity of succulent feed relished by stock. When kept eaten down in the spring, and not allowed to become rank, it affords good feed for a considerable length of time.

235. *Microlæna stipoides*, R. B.—Perennial grass of quick growth, producing abundance of seed, keeps green during the dryest summer, and vegetates freely during the winter, and may be considered a good cattle grass.

236. *Panicum coloratum*, Linn.—An excellent free-seeding summer species, bearing large panicles of dark-coloured seed.

237. *Panicum lævinode*, Lindl.—This very excellent grass was discovered by Sir Thomas Mitchell, during his exploration in 1831. It was considered by him the best grass met with during his journey. It is used by the natives as an article of food, and is gathered by the women in large quantities, and the seeds pounded between stones, mixed with water, are formed into a kind of paste or bread.

238. *Panicum parviflorum*, R. B.—A fine pasture grass, generally met with on ridges. There are two varieties—one with fine spreading panicles, and the other having only one or two very long erect spikelets in its panicle. Both of them are excellent grasses and worthy of cultivation.

239. *Panicum crus-galli*, Linn.—A strong growing grass that affords a large amount of feed to cattle in seasons of scarcity, and is much improved by cultivation.

240. *Panicum decompositum*, R. B.—One of the most valuable of the Darling Downs grasses ; under cultivation this grass has yielded in one season over three tons of hay per acre.

241. *Panicum hispidulum*, Retz.—A rich annual grass, abundant upon the sides of lagoons in Northern Queensland ; this grass is much relished by stock and is well suited for cattle pasture.

242. *Panicum virgatum*, Linn.—A good pasture grass, abundant on open downs country. The seeds of this grass are used at times as an article of food by the natives.

243. *Panicum italicum*, L.—This grass, notwithstanding its specific name, is of Indian origin, and is also a native of Northern Australia. It is a good pasture grass, and possesses fattening properties, and thrives well upon poor dry soils ; although it is an annual it increases quickly, from being an abundant seed-bearer. The seeds, when pounded, mixed with water, and baked, are used as food by the natives.

244. *Poa Brownii*, Nees.—There are several varieties of this fine pasture grass, common on both rich and poor soils, producing an abundance of foliage ; bears hard feeding, and is one of the best grasses to stand both winter and summer.

245. *Poa cæspitosa*, Nees (Weeping Polly Grass).—A fine grass, with rather a tufty habit of growth, generally met with upon rich soils, where it produces freely.

246. *Poa parviflora*, R. B.—Very abundant annual grass, and affords good feed to stock throughout the season.

247. *Poa Chinensis*, Kœnig.—Excellent pasture grass, much relished by stock.

248. *Perotis rara*, R. B.—Good pasture grass, quick grower, and affords succulent feed.
249. *Sporobolus indicus*, R. B.—An excellent pasture grass, generally found upon alluvial soils, and resists drought well.
250. *Sporobolus elongatus*, R. B.—Fine open pasture grass, found throughout the colony. Its numerous penetrating roots enable it to resist severe drought.
251. *Stipa Dichelachne*, Steud.—One of the best winter grasses; quick grower and abundant seeder.
252. *Stipa ramosissima*, Sieb. (Bamboo Grass).—Though apparently a hard grass, it is highly spoken of as horse-feed, and produces a very large quantity of fodder.
253. *Daucus brachiatus*, Sieb. (Native Carrot).
254. *Apium leptophyllum*, F. M. (Wild Parsley).
255. *Plantago varia*, R. B. (Native Plantain). This and the two preceding plants are relished by stock.
256. *Chenopodium auricomum*, Lindl. (Salt-bush).—This and the following are salinous plants possessing wholesome and nutritious properties, much relished by stock, and, in the absence of other sources of salt supply, are essential to their well-doing. Their capabilities of resisting heat and drought are very great, and their cultivation easy.
257. *Rhagodia parabolica*, Br. (Salt-bush).
258. *Atriplex semibaccata*, R. B. (Salt-bush).
259. *Atriplex vesicaria*, Hew. (Salt-bush).
260. *Atriplex*, Spe. (Salt-bush).

By Authority: JAMES C. BEAL, Government Printer, William street, Brisbane.

www.ingramcontent.com/pod-product-compliance
Lightning Source LLC
Chambersburg PA
CBHW020336090426
42735CB00009B/1565